AN ESSAY ON
BELIEF AND ACCEPTANCE

Russ Pannier

12 - 2 - 95

An Essay on
Belief and Acceptance

L. JONATHAN COHEN

CLARENDON PRESS · OXFORD

Oxford University Press, Walton Street, Oxford OX2 6DP

Oxford New York
Athens Auckland Bangkok Bombay
Calcutta Cape Town Dar es Salaam Delhi
Florence Hong Kong Istanbul Karachi
Kuala Lumpur Madras Madrid Melbourne
Mexico City Nairobi Paris Singapore
Taipei Tokyo Toronto
and associated companies in
Berlin Ibadan

Oxford is a trade mark of Oxford University Press

Published in the United States by
Oxford University Press Inc., New York

First published 1992
First issued in paperback 1995

British Library Cataloguing in Publication Data
Data available

Library of Congress Cataloging in Publication Data
Cohen, L. Jonathan (Laurence Jonathan)
An essay on belief and acceptance / L. Jonathan Cohen.
Includes index.
1. Knowledge, Theory of. 2. Belief and doubt. 3. Philosophy of
mind. 4. Cognition. I. Title.
BD161.C633 1992 121'.6—dc20 92-8704
ISBN 0-19-824294-8
ISBN 0-19-823604-2 (Pbk)

Printed in Great Britain by
Bookcraft (Bath) Ltd,
Midsomer Norton, Avon

For
My Grandchildren

PREFACE

In the preparation of this book I have been much helped by discussions which took place on various occasions during 1988–91 after I had read papers connected with the book's topic—in particular at Columbia, Illinois (Champain-Urbana), McGill, New York, Northwestern, Notre Dame, Oxford, Rutgers, Toronto, and York Universities, at the Cambridge Applied Psychology Unit, at a workshop on the Philosophy of Probability in Paris, at a conference on Knowledge in Ankara, at the Turing commemorative colloquium in Sussex University, at a conference on Decision and Inference in Litigation at Yeshivah University (Cardozo School of Law), and at the 18th World Congress of Philosophy in Brighton.

I am also very grateful to Neil Cooper, Robert Gay, Margaret Gilbert, John Hyman, Peter Lamarque, James Logue, Ian Maclean, Alvin Plantinga, and Adrian Zuckerman for many helpful comments and criticisms on earlier drafts of substantial parts of the book. I am especially indebted to Jonathan Adler for being able to talk over so many of the issues with him. The reader for Oxford University Press made a number of valuable suggestions about the substance of the book, and the Press's copy-editor (Mrs Dorothy McCarthy) supplied a lot of useful advice on points of style. Finally I must acknowledge my appreciation of the great care with which successive parts of the book were typed by Pat Lloyd and Ann Shackle.

For stylistic considerations, and where the intended sense is quite clear, I have sometimes avoided drawing an explicit distinction between the use and the mention of a term. Also, unless there are contextual reasons to suppose otherwise, the pronoun 'he' is to be understood in the text as meaning 'he or she', the pronoun 'him' as meaning 'him or her', and the pronoun 'his' as meaning 'his or her'.

I published an earlier version of some of the ideas in the book in 'Belief and Acceptance', *Mind* 98 (1989), pp. 367–89. Parts of §§19–20 appeared in 'Should a Jury Say what it Believes or what it Accepts, *Cardozo Law Review* 13 (1991), pp. 465–83.

L. J. C.

28 November 1991

CONTENTS

I
What is the Difference?

Is cognition an active or a passive process? To resolve this old dispute, it is first necessary to distinguish clearly the concept of acceptance from the concept of belief (§1). And this distinction needs to be glossed by our emphasizing (§2) that belief is a disposition, not an occurrent feeling; that normally some relevant thought or experience is required to trigger activation of the disposition; that belief is a disposition to feel that p, not to say, or act as if it were the case, that p; that there are quite a variety of such credal feelings; that acceptance, in this connection, is a mental act or policy, not a speech-act; that acceptance is not the same as supposition, assumption, presumption or hypothesizing; that a person can activate two beliefs simultaneously, but cannot explicitly accept them simultaneously; that both belief and acceptance can be exercised in relation to normative issues as well as to matters of fact; and that the distinction proposed here is not to be confused with certain other distinctions that have been drawn recently. There is a natural tendency (§3) for states of belief that p to be associated with policies of acceptance that p and vice versa, but it is always conceptually possible for one of the two to exist without the other. Indeed it is clear that (§4) acceptance is voluntary and belief involuntary. It is also clear that (§5) from a subjective point of view acceptance is closed under deducibility, while belief is not, and that (§6) acceptance also needs to be compared with belief in regard to a number of other logical properties.

§1. THE CONCEPTUAL NATURE OF THE DISTINCTION

There is an old dispute in Western philosophy about whether the human mind is passive or active in the process of acquiring canonical knowledge concerning the facts and laws of Nature. According to Descartes we articulate such knowledge in voluntary judgements whereby we either assent to or dissent from some relevant mental representation. Thus each item of conscious knowledge is gained through an act of free-will, and any thought that is admitted or accepted may also be rejected if there is reason to doubt it.[1] But according to Hume we learn about Nature via the formation of beliefs, there is no presentation of cognitive options, and so belief 'depends not on the will'. Indeed, on his view 'belief is nothing but a peculiar feeling' that is 'different from what attends the mere *reveries* of the imagination'.[2] So on Hume's view our knowledge of Nature is not acquired by voluntary acts of cognitive judgement, as Descartes held, but by the involuntary growth of cognitive feelings. Later Kant took up and enriched the activist theme, with his detailed exploration of the thesis[3] that knowledge always involves spontaneity of conception alongside the receptivity of impressions. And on the other side Humeans, like J. S. Mill, continued to treat cognition as the domain of causal laws that explain how our mental feelings originate or how one passive state produces another.[4]

In twentieth-century analytical philosophy this old dispute has largely remained dormant, while the main conceptual distinction that is necessary for stating the point at issue has tended to lose its sharpness. Sometimes conditions for the rationality of belief (which is a passive state) have been treated indistinguishably from conditions for the rationality of acceptance (which is an active policy).[5] Sometimes 'acceptance' has been said to be actually a label for the presence of belief as distinct from its absence.[6] Sometimes belief has been attributed the very quality of voluntariness that used to be contrasted with it.[7] Sometimes belief has been discussed *ad nauseam* without any mention at all of acceptance.[8] Sometimes

[1] R. Descartes, *The Philosophical Works*, trans. E. S. Haldane and G. R. T. Ross, vol. i (Cambridge: Cambridge University Press, 1931), pp. 144–5, cf. pp. 235–6.

[2] D. Hume, *A Treatise of Human Nature*, ed. L. A. Selby-Bigge (Oxford: Clarendon Press, 1888), p. 624, cf. p. 183.

[3] I. Kant, *Critique of Pure Reason*, trans. N. Kemp Smith (London: Macmillan, 1950), pp. 92–3. See also T. Reid, *Works*, ed. Sir W. Hamilton, 8th edn. (Edinburgh: James Thin, 1895), i. 115.

[4] J. S. Mill, *A System of Logic, Ratiocinative and Inductive* (London: Macmillan, 1950), pp. 92–3.

[5] For example, I. Levi, *Decisions and Revisions, Philosophical Essays on Knowledge and Value* (Cambridge: Cambridge University Press, 1984), p. 15; H. E. Kyburg, 'Rational Belief', *The Behavioural and Brain Sciences*, 6 (1983), p. 236.

[6] For example, A. I. Goldman, *Epistemology and Cognition* (Cambridge, Mass.: Harvard University Press, 1986), p. 324; P. Maher, 'The Irrelevance of Belief to Rational Action', *Erkenntnis*, 24 (1986), p. 363.

[7] B. van Fraassen, 'Belief and the Will', *Journal of Philosophy*, 81 (1984), pp. 235–56.

[8] Recent examples are W. J. Rapaport, 'Logical Foundations for Belief Representation', *Cognitive Science*, 10 (1986), pp. 371–422; and F. Dretske, *Explaining Behaviour* (Cambridge, Mass.: MIT Press, 1988).

belief has instead been denied existence and the concept of belief held a useless figment of folk psychology, so that the classical issue can no longer be raised.[9]

It turns out, however, that there is considerable mileage to be gained from a sharp restatement of the underlying distinction in modern terms. Specifically a satisfactory differentiation between belief and acceptance is crucial to the resolution of problems about explanations in terms of reasons or purposes, problems about Moore's paradox and the difference between statement and assertion, problems about the optimal structure of scientific knowledge and judicial fact-finding, problems about the nature of subjective probability, problems about the relationship of intellectual intuitions to normative doctrines, problems about the paradoxes of self-deception and *akrasia*, and many other problems about connected issues. It is this width of application that makes recognition of the distinction so important. An epistemology that does not at some point explore the differing roles of active and passive cognition is radically defective. Indeed, without pursuit of the distinction into its many implications and applications, we cannot even apprehend the conceptual resources of contemporary folk psychology—i.e. of common-sense talk about the mind—let alone pass judgement on them.

In the present chapter I shall try to trace out the main lines of the distinction that needs to be drawn, and in subsequent chapters I shall apply this distinction to various familiar philosophical issues that it can help to clarify. Indeed, to the extent that the central distinction and each of its applications can be shown to be inherently reasonable they also reinforce one another. The validity of each of them is enhanced by the cumulative impact of the whole, as it becomes evident that none of them is just an *ad hoc* stratagem. But in each problem-area I shall concentrate on the work to be done by applying the central distinction, rather than wander into the complexities of adjacent issues.

The fundamental difference that needs to be characterized is not *just* a socio-historical fact—a difference of meaning, in relevant contexts, between the words 'believe' and 'accept'. It is not *just* a feature of English (or French, or German) linguistic idiom or of so-called 'ordinary' or 'folk-psychological' language in general. Rather, it is a conceptual difference that needs to be marked somehow, whatever the vocabulary employed to mark it. But the words 'believe' and 'accept' as I shall employ them are not technical terms either. The meanings in which I use them are in fact recognizably identical with those that they very often, and perhaps standardly, have in non-philosophical usage, wherever they introduce clauses in indirect discourse. That is to say, I am concerned with contexts that have a grammatical structure similar to 'He believes that it is raining' or 'She accepts that the train will be late today', rather than to 'She believes in hard work', 'They believe him', 'She accepts responsibility', or 'He accepts compliments gracefully'. And I shall sometimes be invoking linguistic intuitions appropriate to the former type of context in order to support my analyses.

My initial clarification of these meanings will have three stages. First, I shall summarize them in a very few sentences, so as to give some rough indication of the direction in which the discussion is headed. Secondly, I shall introduce some glosses on these summaries in order to prevent possible misunderstandings at the outset. Thirdly, I shall draw attention to some crucial features of the concepts so characterized, and these features will help to substantiate the distinction.

§2. HOW TO CARVE IT AT THE JOINT

First then, and very briefly, belief that p is a disposition, when one is attending to issues raised, or items referred to, by the proposition that p, normally to feel it true that p and false that *not-p*, whether or not one is willing to act, speak, or reason accordingly. But to accept the proposition or rule of inference that p is to treat it as given that p. More precisely, to accept that p is to have or adopt a policy of deeming, positing, or postulating that p—i.e. of including that proposition or rule among one's premises for deciding what to do or think in a particular context, whether or not one feels it to be true that p. The standard way to discover whether you yourself believe that p is by introspecting whether you are normally disposed to feel that p when you consider the issue. And you answer another person's question whether you believe that p by reporting whether you are so disposed. But you answer the question whether you accept that *p* by forming or reporting an intention about the foundations of your proofs, arguments, reasonings, or deliberations. By acquiring new beliefs you widen the range of feelings that you are disposed to have. By acceptance you increase your stock of premissable data and employable rules of inference. So belief that *p* can coexist in your mind with acceptance that *p*. But it is not conceptually tied to doing so.

There you have the heart of the matter. That is where the concepts of belief and acceptance need to be prised apart from one another. That is how you can carve them at the joint. Belief is a disposition to feel, acceptance a policy for reasoning. 'Belief' carries no conceptual implications about reasoning, 'acceptance' carries none about feelings.

But, as a second stage, some elucidatory glosses are certainly needed.

Gloss no. 1. Belief is a disposition, not an occurrent feeling. Although, when you listen, you can hear the relentless downpour through the curtains, you may from time to time stop thinking about the rain. But you do not then stop believing that it is raining—as presumably you would do if belief were an occurrent feeling. Moreover, though many beliefs only commence at the time of their first being felt, there are many others that apparently antedate this, just as by being dried in the sun a lump of clay may become brittle long before pressure is applied and it breaks. Thus, if you have long believed that London is larger than Oxford and that Oxford is larger than St Andrews, then you will most probably (though not necessarily—see §5 below) have long believed that London is larger than St Andrews, even if the belief has never explicitly occurred to you until you were asked. Indeed, even if you have never consciously believed anything implying that London is larger than St Andrews, your answer to the question 'Do you believe that London is larger than St Andrews?' would most probably still be 'Yes'. That is to say, a present feeling that London is larger than St Andrews would be taken to display a pre-existing disposition to feel this. How could you not have such a disposition if you have visited both London and St Andrews and remember— even quite roughly—what they were like?[10] People can say about

---

[10] *Pace* A. I. Goldman, *Epistemology and Cognition* (Cambridge, Mass.: Harvard University Press, 1986), p. 202.

you without self-contradiction, 'He almost certainly believes it, even if he has never yet consciously thought about it.' Why should you have thought about it, if there was no occasion for you to do so? And, after all, at any one time almost all a person's beliefs have to be absent from his current consciousness, since no more than a few such dispositions can be activated at any one time. It follows that when you die you may have had quite a number of beliefs that were never activated. No doubt our vocabulary could include a term denoting a disposition to feel that a specified proposition is true which applies only to dispositions that are sometimes activated. But 'belief' is not such a term.

On the other hand, some beliefs last only a very short while, and may perhaps be displayed throughout that period, as when one suddenly comes to believe that a gun has been fired, a moment later realizes that it was a car backfiring, and then forgets the matter altogether. The brevity of such an occurrence is not a reason for denying that a belief has come and gone (*pace* Kent Bach[11]). Compare other dispositions: the sheet of glass that was smashed as soon as it was manufactured was certainly fragile even though it did not exist for long. Nor should the fact that some beliefs are concurrent with their activations tempt us to identify the one with the other. Such a concurrence, where it occurs, is a contingent, not a necessary, feature.

So belief is not a habit, as Peirce took it to be.[12] Habits cannot exist before they are exercised, in the way that, as we have just seen, a belief-disposition can exist before it is activated. Nor can habits last as briefly, on the human time-scale, as belief-dispositions can. No human habit can be as brief as the time taken to form the belief that a gun has been fired and then to realize that a car was backfiring. Nor is the strength of a belief like the strength of a habit. If your belief varies in strength, it varies in accordance with the intensity of your feeling that p when your disposition to feel that p is activated. But habits vary in strength in accordance with

[11] K. Bach, 'An Analysis of Self-Deception', *Philosophy and Phenomenological Research*, 41 (1981), pp. 354–7.

[12] C. S. Peirce, *Collected Papers*, ed. C. Hartshorne and P. Weiss (Cambridge, Mass.: Harvard University Press, 1934), v. 230, 330, and elsewhere. But Peirce came closer to the correct position when he distinguished between judgement accompanied by 'a peculiar feeling or conviction' and judgement 'from which a man will act', ibid. p. 148.

their capacity to persist, rather like your disposition to feel that p may vary in the firmness or stability with which you are so disposed.

Bogdan[13] has suggested that belief that p is an attitude to the information that p rather than just a disposition to feel it true that p. On this view belief tracks the receipt of information and is therefore in part delimited by relevant parameters of incrementation. And on Bogdan's view it follows, as he points out, that we do not continue to believe that p while we are asleep or inattentive but may manufacture that belief again, if and when occasion demands, by the retrieval of relevant stored information. However, what Bogdan says about incrementation fits acceptance better than it fits belief. So far as acceptance that p involves adopting the policy of taking it as a premiss that p, acceptance does indeed register an increment of information. In this respect the initial act of adopting the policy of positing that p may be contrasted with the process of forming the belief that p, while *having* the policy of positing that p is what should be contrasted with believing that p. Even then there is no basis here for supposing that either a policy of positing that p, or a belief that p, is normally conceived to go out of existence each time the believer falls asleep or ceases to attend to the issue. Nor should they be so conceived. If for two years you have believed, or accepted, that p, it doesn't follow that you haven't slept for two years.

Gloss no. 2. I have said that belief that p is a disposition *normally* to feel that p, and the point of this hedging needs to be clarified. What normally triggers activation of the disposition is the mental state of thinking about whether it is the case that p, of thinking about something referred to by the proposition that p, or of thinking about some other such connected issue, or of having a related experience. But, even when one or other of these conditions is satisfied, feelings that would have exemplified the belief that p sometimes do not occur. They may fail to arise at the moment because you have difficulty in remembering that p or because you need or want to concentrate on other relevant matters. Or they may just be crowded out because you have too many relevant beliefs for them all to be activated within the same span of

[13] R. J. Bogdan, 'The Manufacture of Belief', in R. J. Bogdan (ed.), *Belief: Form, Content and Function* (Oxford: Clarendon Press, 1986), pp. 149–84.

consideration. Or occurrence of the feeling that p may be blocked at the outset by some accidental distraction. And not only are there thus various abnormal kinds of circumstances in which a belief fails to be activated when it would normally be. It may also succeed in getting activated even though none of the normal kinds of trigger is operative, as when a familiar belief suddenly, but quite irrelevantly, flashes before the mind.

Gloss no. 3. Belief is a disposition normally to feel that things are thus-or-so, not a disposition to say that they are or to act accordingly (*pace* Ryle, Geach, and others[14]).

Of course, some people are so talkative that they apparently try to tell you every belief they have, and perhaps every other feeling too, unless there is some special reason for keeping it to themselves or you manage to extricate yourself from their garrulousness. But others are reticent to the point of secrecy, unless there is some special reason for disclosure, and they may have just as many beliefs and other feelings. It may well be a psychological fact that most human belief-feelings are embodied in linguistic utterances, even if only in sub-vocal ones. But this is not required a priori by the analysis of the concept of belief. Otherwise infants and animals could not have beliefs (see §9 below). Nor could beliefs occur faster than speech, as when one driver almost instantaneously grasps the intentions of another. Moreover, belief is not at all like a disposition to bet that so-and-so is the case.[15] Some people are such gamblers that they will offer you odds on the truth of each belief that they have. But others are so averse to risk that they would never offer you odds on anything. Yet they too have beliefs. So having a disposition to speak and act as if one feels that p is not a necessary condition for believing that p.

Nor is it a sufficient condition. By speaking and acting as if he feels that p, a person may be trying to deceive others into thinking that he believes that p, even though he actually has no such belief. Pretended belief has to be distinguished from real belief. And

---

[14] G. Ryle, *The Concept of Mind* (London: Hutchinson, 1949), p. 175; P. T. Geach, *Mental Acts: Their Content and Their Objects* (London: Routledge and Kegan Paul, 1957), p. 8.

[15] As suggested by R. B. de Sousa, 'How to Give a Piece of Your Mind, or the Logic of Belief and Assent', *Review of Metaphysics*, xxxv (1971), pp. 52–79, and by D. C. Dennett, *The Intentional Stance* (Cambridge, Mass.: MIT Press, 1989), p. 19 (footnote).

though pretences are often deliberate some people just can't help making them. Nor does belief that p necessarily accompany a disposition to lay an odds-on bet that p. There are many other reasons for betting at this or that odds than to display one's beliefs (see §19 below).

Note that the kinds of mental feelings or experiences to which believers are characteristically disposed belong in the same overall category as manifestations of hopes-that, fears-that, joys-that, desires-that, embarrassments-that, disappointments-that, bitter-ness-that, etc. They all have propositional objects (by which I mean that their content is reported in indirect discourse). And our credal feelings, like our emotional ones, may be revealed to others, not only in speech but also by incidental grimaces, pallors, blushes, vocal ejaculations, intakes of breath, hand-gestures, body move-ments and attitudes, etc. Indeed, they may also be revealed by a person's actions, in the light of his known desires, aversions, etc. If a person is known to want access through a locked door and is seen to insert a key in the door, we would often infer that he occurrently believes the key to be the right one to open the door. But again one should remember that there are other people, with just as many beliefs, who are more disposed to conceal some of those beliefs—whether in speech or in action or in both—than to reveal them, just as they may be disposed to conceal some of their emotions.

Perhaps there is an understandable temptation to argue here that belief that p must be not only a disposition to have certain feelings, but also a disposition to speak and act accordingly, because we must certainly admit that, *if* a person were not reticent or secretive, he would so speak or act. But this argument is untenable since it presupposes that the truth of any such subjunctive conditional establishes the existence of the corresponding disposition—as if a sheet of ordinary glass may be said to have a non-fragile disposition since it would not break if it were kept free from any impact or pressure. And the conditions on which the activation of a disposi-tion would depend cannot be taken to include the absence of those conditions on which the activation of the opposite disposition would depend, since then it would always be possible to ascribe opposite dispositions to the same thing at the same time. Indeed we have to assume that, if something has a disposition to behave thus-or-so when it is treated in such-and-such a way, it must have some feature that so disposes it. Thus a sheet of ordinary glass is fragile because of its molecular structure. And perhaps we shall one day find out just what features of the brain dispose us to have credal feelings in appropriate circumstances. But there seems no reason to suppose that some such features dispose everyone to reveal their beliefs to others. Instead we must distinguish between the disposition to execute certain utterances and actions, which is normally but not necessarily a sign of a person's belief, and the disposition to have certain feelings, which is what constitutes the belief. It is normally, but not always, by discovering a disposition of the former kind that we can infer one of the latter.

In other words, even if we grant that a person is normally disposed to speak and act in accordance with his credal feelings— i.e. to do this if he has the opportunity and if doing so furthers the achievement of his desires—it does not follow that his disposition constitutes a part of the belief. The disposition to speak and act accordingly may normally accompany any disposition to have certain credal feelings, without that companionship's being necessary to constitute a state of belief.

Moreover, there is a strong reason to suppose that any connection between the two dispositions is in fact a contingent one. Consider what is involved in a person's appearing to have a belief that not-p while in reality he secretly believes that p. Perhaps by carrying an umbrella he appears to believe that the dry weather will not continue, while in reality he believes that it will continue and carries the umbrella as a decorous means of self-defence. Such a person acts on appropriate occasions as if he is firmly disposed to feel that not-p. Indeed, he may truthfully be said to have taken on a firm disposition to act in this way. So he cannot at the same time have a disposition to act as if he is disposed to feel that p. Such a case certainly illustrates the contingency of the connection that exists in normal cases between a person's disposition to feel that p and his disposition to speak and act as if he feels that p.

Finally it ought not to go unremarked that there is a radical asymmetry between those two dispositions so far as their relationship to belief is concerned. Consider someone who has a disposition to feel that p and lacks the disposition to speak and act accordingly. You can hardly deny that he believes that p, even if you may never know of such a reticent person unless he is yourself. But if you heard of a person who has a disposition to speak and act as if he is disposed to feel that *p*, though in fact he is not disposed to feel that *p*, you would not say that he believes that *p*. You would say instead that he appears—misleadingly—to believe that *p*.

Gloss no. 4. There is quite a variety of mental feelings or gut reactions that may pertain to a person's state of belief on a particular issue. Despair, incredulity, disbelief, doubt, uncertainty, suspicion, surprise, intuition, impression, fear, expectation, persuasion, faith, confidence, conviction, etc. all involve credal feelings that we experience from time to time in reflecting on this or that proposition that somehow comes before our mind. If the feelings in which normal levels of belief display themselves are less noticed or noticeable than those in which more extreme states are displayed, that is presumably because they are a great deal more familiar. Compare how we often hardly notice our familiar physical surroundings, even though we do not cease to see them. Similarly we are hardly aware of many familiar desires—like the desire to cross the road—as issuing in *feelings*. Yet they belong in much the same category as longings, yearnings, covetings, hankerings, lustings, and cravings.

Feeling it true that *p* may thus be compared with feeling it good that *p*. All credal feelings, whether weak or strong, share the distinctive feature of constituting some kind of orientation on the 'True or false?' issue in relation to their propositional objects, whereas affective mental feelings, like those of anger or desire, constitute some kind of orientation on the 'Good or bad?' issue. But there is a close connection between these two types of feeling in certain cases. A person's feelings about the truth of ethical or value-related propositions are normally expected to indicate his feelings about the behaviour with which such propositions are concerned. He would be regarded as a potential victim of what Aristotle called *akrasia* (see §§26–7) if he believed that taking bribes is morally bad but nevertheless felt attracted to take them.

Intellectualist philosophers may be inclined to object here that only the 'Good or bad?' issue, and not the 'True or false?' one, is suited to be a topic for feelings. Feelings are relevant, they may say, to the question whether it is right for the world to be made to fit a certain description, not to the question whether such-or-such a description is right for the world as it is. They would then presumably imply that the sense in which people speak of 'feeling' that it is true that *p* is a figurative, not a literal, one.

But how could it be shown that it is figurative? It is certainly not a metaphor peculiar to English or to the English literary tradition. Indeed to declare a 'feeling' of doubt or surprise that *p* seems linguistically quite on a par with declaring a 'feeling' of disgust that *p*.

What is important here is not to provide a phrase that is a synonymous equivalent for the word 'belief', but to place belief in its right conceptual category. Specifically, it is classifiable as a disposition to have a certain kind of mental feeling, not as a disposition to perform a certain kind of action.

Gloss no. 5. The word 'accept' is often used to signify the speech-act of assent whereby a person may orally (or in writing) agree to the truth of a proposition whether or not this oral (or written) agreement accords with his actual state of mind. But the sense with which I am primarily concerned is the one in which this word signifies a mental act, or a pattern, system, or policy of mental action, rather than a speech-act. What a person accepts, like what he believes, may in practice be reflected in how he speaks or behaves. But it does not have to be. The acceptance may be tacit. Nevertheless in the case of acceptance, though not of belief (see *Gloss no. 3* above), there is an a priori conceptual requirement that what is under consideration is tied to some type of linguistic formulation even if this formulation is never uttered aloud. Premisses and rules of inference have to be conceived in linguistic terms: feelings do not. That is how logic can get to grips with inference and formulate its principles as rules for linguistic transformation. And it is also why, though animals and pre-linguistic infants can be credited with beliefs, they cannot be credited with acceptances (as will be argued in §§10 and 14 below).

Gloss no. 6. Our reasons for accepting that it will rain this evening may be prudential rather than evidential. So too may our reasons be for supposing, assuming, presuming, or hypothesizing this. But acceptance is not the same as supposition, assumption, presumption, or hypothesizing, in the standard senses of those terms. Thus the verb 'to suppose' commonly denotes an inherently temporary act of imagination, as in 'Let's suppose we're on a desert island', whereas acceptance implies commitment to a pattern, system, or policy—whether long or short term—of premissing that *p* as a basis for a decision. So, if you describe yourself as supposing that *p*, you imply that you don't know that *p* (since if you do know you would be expected to say so). But you don't imply this if you describe yourself as accepting that *p*. Again, acceptance, like assumption, may be relative to a particular context of reasoning. For example, what we accept as a premiss for resolving conflicts of duty in our professional concerns, we may not wish to accept also as a premiss for resolving conflicts of duty in family life. But making an assumption is an inherently makeshift manœuvre, even within its particular context. For example, we can act on the assumption that *p* in order to test whether it is true that *p*. A mathematician may investigate in this way whether there is a *reductio ad absurdum* proof for not-*p*, for example, and if he is successful (and derives an obvious contradiction from *p*) it is not-*p* rather than *p* that will be accepted. Or a counter-espionage operative may feed information to a suspect on the assumption that he is an enemy agent in order to test whether he is indeed one, and only when the assumption is confirmed (by onward passage of the information) will it be accepted as a premiss for future strategy. Often too we are restricted to assuming that *p* for the moment, just because we don't at the moment have enough evidence to adopt the policy of premissing that *p*. Or maybe we say that we are only assuming that *p* in order to point out that it is arbitrary whether we take *p* or some other such proposition as our premiss in the given context. Again, a presumption is typically what you may take for granted about a particular issue, in default of reasons against so doing. But for acceptance that *p* to be justifiable you normally need to have reasons in favour of it. And, though a hypothesis may, if confirmed, or *faute de mieux*, end up by being accepted, it always begins as a mere assumption or supposition.

Fundamentally, the term 'acceptance' suggests a (posited) giver of premisses or rules of inference as well as a (positing) receiver, where the giver may be perceived reality (as when you look out of the window and accept that it is raining), or a code of ethics (as when a dealer in the City of London accepts that he should honour a spoken undertaking), or some analogous source of data. But the terms 'assume', 'suppose', 'presume', and 'hypothesize' make no such suggestion. Assumptions, suppositions, presumptions, or hypotheses are ways of premissing that do not need to hang on anything beyond themselves.

Note too how acceptance is related to relevance in a way that assumptions, suppositions, hypotheses, or presumptions are not.

You hold it relevant in a given context that p if and only if you hold that in this context anyone should accept that p, i.e. if and only if you hold that in this context anyone should adopt the policy of taking the proposition that p as a premiss for his proofs, arguments, reasonings, or deliberations. And in a given context you hold it more relevant that p than that q if and only if you hold it more important in that context to accept that p than that q. But you would often be mistaken if you held it relevant that p merely because you held that anyone should assume, suppose, hypothesize, or presume that p. For you may hold that anyone should do this just because assuming, supposing, or hypothesizing that p is part of the normal procedure for investigating whether it is indeed relevant that p, or because presuming that p is the proper or polite thing to do in the circumstances.

Nor is acceptance that p the same as speaking and acting as if it is true that p. When the terrorists have thrown their first hand-grenade you may gladly accept, as you lie on the floor, that you can still move your limbs. But, if you are wise, you will act in that context as if you are dead or paralysed, not as if you can still speak or move your limbs. And, if George accepts that it is desirable for him to deceive Mary, he should—normally—speak and act as if it is not desirable for him to deceive her. Equally acting as if it is true that p is not necessarily a way of declaring that you accept that p. For, when you act as if you are dead, you are certainly not declaring that you accept that you are dead: dead people cannot make any declarations at all about the premisses that they are adopting. So what is correct is just that, when you really do accept the proposition that p as a premiss for your deliberations, then the decisions in which those deliberations issue will be decisions that are, *ceteris paribus*, appropriate to that acceptance.

Gloss no. 7. Because they are feelings, the manifestations of two or more beliefs may sometimes be thought of as occurring simultaneously. You may in principle feel at the very same moment that you are smelling smoke, that the room is getting rather hot, and that flames are flickering up through the floor-boards. Indeed, the synchronous combination of these feelings may cause you to rush to the fire-escape. But to be said to premiss each of such facts explicitly (in virtue of your accepting their reality), you must be supposed to pay attention to them sequentially, however rapidly your thoughts about them follow one another.

Gloss no. 8. Modern philosophers have tended, like Hume, to confine their conception of belief to beliefs about matters of empirical fact. But in the senses considered here neither the word 'belief' nor the word 'acceptance' need be so confined in its range of reference. A person can feel it to be true, when the question arises, that child-sacrifice is morally wrong (see *Gloss no. 4* above), or that 97 is a prime number, or that 'London is larger than St Andrews' may be inferred from 'London is larger than Oxford' and 'Oxford is larger than St Andrews', just as readily as he feels it true, on an appropriate occasion, that it is now raining. Such feelings about normative a priori issues are sometimes attributed to specialized faculties of conscience, intuition, etc. But it is convenient to classify them generically as manifestations of beliefs, in order to draw attention to the existence of a difference between belief and acceptance on these issues that parallels the difference on factual issues. For you can certainly accept a normative principle—in the sense of adopting a policy of going along with it as a premiss for practical reasoning—whether or not that principle is endorsed by your credal feelings of conscience or intuition. And, after carefully checking each step of a long mathematical proof, you can accept its validity as a whole even though you have no intuitive conviction of this. Nor in such matters is acceptance any more required to coexist with belief than it is in regard to factual issues. You can feel a normative principle to be right whether or not you actually accept it in practice as an overriding maxim for action. People do not always conform their practical maxims to their consciences or intuitions. Not everyone is prepared to stand out against the conventional ethics of their community, for example. And Aristotle's discussion of what he called *akrasia* is also relevant here (see §§26–8 below).

Gloss no. 9. Dennett's distinction[16] between belief and what he calls 'opinion'—which builds on an earlier distinction of de Sousa's[17] between belief and assent—resembles the distinction between belief and acceptance in certain respects. Like acceptance, opinion differs from belief in being a mental state that has to be active rather than passive, linguistically formulatable, not available

[16] D. Dennett, *Brainstorms: Philosophical Essays on Mind and Psychology* (Hassocks: Harvester Press, 1979), pp. 300–9.
[17] In 'How to Give a Piece of Your Mind.'

to animals, and not a matter of degree. But, while opinion, according to Dennett, arises only through a change of mind, people in practice often accept views about issues on which they have never previously reflected and therefore have nothing about which to change their minds. Also acceptance, unlike opinion, may be relative to context, although it is certainly possible to treat some premisses as being acceptable in any context whatever. More importantly, opinion, in Dennett's sense of the word, is not tied to premissing. As a result the concept of opinion, unlike that of acceptance (see §§8–20 below), is not of much use in clarifying the difference between reasons and causes in purposive explanation, or the foundations of Moore's paradox, or the requirements for scientific knowledge, or the make-up of self-deceit, or the structure of philosophical reasoning. Nor, indeed, is it applied by Dennett to those tasks.

Lehrer[18] has argued that a person may accept what he believes or what he does not believe and may refuse to accept what he does believe. But Lehrer defines the acceptance of a proposition in this context as assenting to it when one's only purpose is to assent to what is true and to refuse to assent to what is false. And here again there is no tie-up between accepting and premissing. Consequently acceptance for prudential, ethical, or other non-evidential reasons is excluded altogether, and the distinction drawn does not have much potential for clarifying epistemological issues concerned with premissing.

§3. SOME CONNECTIONS AND DISCONNECTIONS
BETWEEN THE TWO MENTAL STATES

Belief and acceptance, when understood in the way that I have characterized, certainly resemble one another in some important features. Both are mental states that can be either fickle or fixed, either about what is or about what ought to be, and either for good reasons or bad reasons or for no conscious or evident reasons at all (see further §12 below). Indeed, it is often difficult to know

---

[18] K. Lehrer, 'The Gettier Problem and the Analysis of Knowledge', in G. S. Pappas (ed.), *Justification and Knowledge: New Studies in Epistemology* (Dordrecht: Reidel, 1979), pp. 65–78.

whether to classify a particular person's mental attitude towards a particular proposition at a particular time as one of belief, of acceptance, or of both. It is often difficult to know whether belief or acceptance has been paramount even in one's own mind. And there seems to be a natural tendency for the two to run together. If you believe that p, it is normal for you also to take that proposition as a premiss, and if you accept that p it is normal for you to feel it true that p. Indeed, there are readily intelligible reasons why we do normally believe what we accept and accept what we believe.

On the one hand, having a belief that p can often be taken to be some at least prima facie reason for accepting that p, even though it may well not be the only, or the best, or even a sufficient, reason. This holds good wherever there is at least a presumption, which may be rebuttable in appropriate circumstances, that a belief would not have arisen at all without there having been some data in its favour. It is unnecessary to invoke here the processes of Darwinian evolution as the ultimate basis for such a presumption, or to appeal instead to the providential care of an all-powerful Deity. (Some people believe in neither.) The fact is that in deciding on what to accept we often need to presume that our subconscious belief-inducing mechanisms—and especially those of perception and memory—have operated veridically, as they normally have done in similar situations in the past, because there may be no time, or no opportunity, to check them consciously in the present situation. If, while driving along a country road, you believe that through a gap in the hedgerow you saw the helmet of a motorcyclist riding the crown of the road towards you round the S-bend, you need to accept that belief as the basis for immediate action. It fits no familiar pattern of illusion. So you need to steer out of the way fast and without any pause for further investigation. And if, when you consult your memory, you believe that you left your keys in the kitchen, that is certainly a reason for your accepting initially that you did leave them there and should therefore look for them there first. Belief is not normally a prima facie reason for acceptance, however, in certain other types of situation. Consider, for example, the situation where what is believed is the existence of such-and-such a causal connection or law of nature. A belief of this kind, that has not been formed on the authority of trusted experts, cries out to be checked before acceptance, in case the experience giving rise to it may have been discoverably unrepresentative in some relevant respect or in case discordant elements in the experience may have been overlooked (see further §22).

Belief that p, on its own, is a conclusive reason for accepting that p only in certain offbeat cases, such as when a person believes that he currently has at least one belief. But our everyday reasonings would be very short of premisses indeed if, in normal cases of perception or memory, we could not treat belief that p as a prima facie reason for accepting that p.

On the other hand, acceptance does quite generally tend to promote belief. Not that acceptance that p can ever be taken as a reason for believing that p. For if it could be so taken we should be in the absurd position of being able at will to manufacture a reason for believing anything, simply by deciding to take it as a premiss. (There is a definite asymmetry here between belief's normally being a reason for acceptance and acceptance's never being a reason for belief.) But acceptance that p very often *causes* belief that p—in the long run if not in the short run. Thus Pascal urged his readers to act in accordance with Catholic doctrine—that is, to take it as a premiss for their practical decisions—since such a policy would tend eventually to induce belief that the doctrine was true.[19] And in everyday matters the very same observed puddle, say, that persuades a driver to accept that the road surface needs mending may also thereby cause him to believe this. Indeed, we often telescope the description of such a process by saying that the puddle persuaded him to believe that the road surface needed mending.

The existence of this natural tendency for states of belief and acceptance to be linked together in everyday experience is probably the main factor in generating the widespread tendency to confound the two concepts with one another in philosophical reflection. If attention is paid only to the combined state, a single label will apparently serve and it will then be of no importance whether the word 'belief' be used as that label or the word 'acceptance' or, as was once commoner among philosophers than now, the word 'judgement'. Moreover, this combined state is liable to be ascribed a misleadingly confused amalgam of relevant characteristics, so that—depending on the amalgams chosen—a variety of philosophical antinomies can be generated, as will be made apparent in the following chapters. With one choice of characteristics, for example,

---

[19] B. Pascal, *Pensées*, trans. J. Warrington (London: Dent, 1960), pp. 95–6.

belief is arguably voluntary: with another, involuntary. With one choice, knowledge that p seems to depend on how belief that p is caused: with another, on whether it is justified. And so on.

But there are a number of special contexts in which belief and acceptance are not in fact expected to coincide, or in which strength of belief that p and degree of inclination to accept that p may vary independently. Some of these contexts are of considerable epistemological importance and will be discussed in the following chapters. Others are more humdrum and can be mentioned briefly here. Both kinds of context testify to the indispensability of the underlying distinction.

One common case is when in learning a skill, and acquiring fluency in its exercise, we pass from accepting what has to be done to believing it. A detailed acceptance of appropriate instructions eventually promotes a corresponding disposition to *feel* what has to be done at any particular point of the skill's operation. That way, for example, a driver becomes able to feel the coexistence of several different requirements. Perhaps he needs at the same time to depress his car's clutch pedal, move his gear lever forward, relax pressure on his accelerator, and turn the steering wheel to the left. But, if he were still at the stage of *accepting* each requirement as taught by his instructor, he would have to do so sequentially.

More generally we can say that, though a person who accepts nothing that he believes is intellectually self-paralysed, a person who habitually accepts everything that he believes is recklessly uncritical. One often needs to go through some process of checking or monitoring the relevant facts in order to determine whether acceptance is justifiable and such a process may well reveal deviant elements in the genesis of the belief. Visual illusion, mishearing, linguistic misunderstanding, numerical miscalculation, misinformation from others, and many other such factors may have played their part in generating a belief that does not deserve acceptance. Moreover, while such a belief will often cease to exist when found undeserving of acceptance, there are other kinds of belief that may be maintained even though acceptance is thought inappropriate. A person might be convinced that p while nevertheless not accepting the use of that proposition as a premiss for any proofs, deliberations, etc. For example, this sometimes happens with beliefs due to racial or sexist prejudice. Or a person might be allowed access to a highly confidential piece of information only after swearing that he will never take it to be a premiss available for use in his reasonings, even in the privacy of his own mind. And what he has sworn to do is thereafter securely accomplished only if he can avoid exploiting his belief that *p*. Such an oath may be quite difficult to keep, but it is at least intelligible. And the interest here is in the distinguishability of two concepts, not in the degree of ease with which two states of mind may be separated.

Nor is the only possibility of separation the existence of belief without corresponding acceptance. There is also quite a variety of possible situations in which acceptance occurs without the corresponding belief. For example, perhaps you can't believe that your hero is a crook, but the evidence is so strong that you decide to accept it. Or, even when on an orthodox assessment the balance of presently available evidence and other cognitively relevant considerations makes the principle that *p* deserve acceptance within the scientific community, you may still have a hunch that not-*p*. So you quite reasonably accept that *p* while at least half-believing that not-*p*. Or perhaps you accept that *p* out of solidarity with an old friend, or a member of your family, or a person you love, even though there is insufficient evidence to produce or justify a belief that *p*. Or for professional purposes a lawyer might accept that his client is not guilty even though he has no belief about the matter. And because reasons for accepting that *p* can thus be ethical, professional, prudential, religious, aesthetic, or otherwise pragmatic instead of evidential it is obvious that a wide range of other, analogous examples could also be cited.

It is therefore not right to say[20] that a person's speech-act of accepting that *p* is insincere unless he also believes that *p*. Instead your speech-act of accepting that *p* is sincere if and only if you actually do have a policy of taking that proposition as a premiss, and your belief or disbelief that *p* may be quite independent of this.

§4. THE VOLUNTARINESS ISSUE

As Hume long ago observed,[21] belief is involuntary. And, as Williams has rightly added, its involuntariness is not so much a

[20] As is said by B. Williams, *Problems of the Self* (Cambridge: Cambridge University Press, 1973), p. 140.
[21] Hume, *A Treatise of Human Nature*, p. 624.

matter of contingent fact (like the impossibility of blushing at will) as of conceptual interconnection.[22] Beliefs are said to come over you, arise in you, or grow on you, like anger or affection does. You cannot don, raise, or grow them yourself. You can plant them in others, but not in yourself. You may decide to believe a friend, i.e. to trust his word. You may even decide to believe *in* him, i.e. to have confidence in his abilities. You may decide also whether to let your mind dwell on a belief or to try to keep your mind off it, whether to check the evidence for it or to leave it unquestioned, whether to voice it or to keep silent, and whether to act on it or to disregard it. But you cannot decide to believe *that* it will rain tomorrow or *that* it will not. You can, of course, decide to accept that it will, or to accept that it will not. The corresponding belief may then ensue eventually (if you do not already have it), but it may not. If the belief does ensue, you have certainly brought about your own belief. You might even be said to have tried to believe and been successful. But you have achieved your belief indirectly, not directly through deciding to believe.

Moreover, there is a consilience in the argument here. This intuitively cogent thesis that belief is necessarily involuntary both supports and is supported by the earlier thesis (§2) that belief is a disposition to have certain feelings, not a disposition to speak or act in certain ways—since the former type of disposition is always involuntary while the latter is normally voluntary. It makes sense to speak of someone as having decided to change what he is disposed to say, even if in practice he finds this too difficult to achieve. But no one can be said to decide to be disposed to feel one way or another. You cannot decide to feel joyful or suspicious.

Nor is this just an accident of linguistic idiom. Important matters hang on it. For example, dispositions to have particular mental feelings cannot be regarded as adoptable at will if their existence in one person's mind is to count as an argument, as it in fact often does, for another person to execute, or not to execute, some related act that might hurt those feelings. For example, the fact that George feels hurt, if you criticize him, counts as a possible argument for your not criticizing him largely because his disposition to feel hurt in such circumstances is incapable of being generated or discarded at will. And analogous things may be said

[22] Williams, *Problems of the Self*, p. 148.

about George's feeling angry, jealous, or doubtful. Contrariwise, the risk of George's becoming disposed thereby to speak or act against your interests counts as a possible argument for your not offending him largely because he *can* form such a disposition at will.

Acceptance, in contrast with belief, occurs at will, whether by an immediate decision or through a gradually formed intention. This is because at bottom it executes a choice—the accepter's choice of which propositions to take as his premises. Belief is not thought of as being normally achieved at will because it is thought of as being regularly caused in each kind of case by something independent of the believer's immediate choice: factual beliefs are typically reactions to what the believer sees or hears, moral beliefs are normally the welcome or unwelcome dictates of his conscience, intuitive beliefs are the immediate, unreflective, and untutored deliverances of his intellect, and so on. We think of our beliefs as states of mind that are normally responsive to the truth, not to our own decisions. Even when you try to induce belief that *p* by first accepting that *p*, you may fail through no fault of your own. You may even intend that you will thus in the end believe that *p*. But your feelings may just be too recalcitrant. On the other hand, if in your reasonings and deliberations you try to *accept* that *p* and fail, it is normally because you have not tried hard enough to maintain the policy of treating *p* as a premiss or inference-licence. And, while we are here concerned primarily with the difference between belief and acceptance, analogous points can no doubt be made also about the differences between other involuntary cognitive experiences like doubt, perplexity, reverie, suspicion, impression, understanding, etc. on the one side, and other voluntary cognitive acts like investigation, supposition, assumption, reasoning, interpretation, etc. on the other. You may get the impression, for example, from an interview that a candidate for admission to your university has considerable ability. But you may nevertheless be unwilling to attribute such ability to him without knowing his test-scores. Similarly, the difference between simulation of belief and pretence of belief is worth remarking. An animal in danger may involuntarily simulate behaviour appropriate to the false belief that *p* and thus perhaps mislead a predator. But, when a person systematically pretends to believe that *p*, he voluntarily accepts premises that endorse his utterances and actions within the relevant context. So such pretences are impossible for any infant that has not yet reached at least the age at which acts of acceptance begin to be effective (§9).[23]

Moreover, if you are not to act arbitrarily or irrationally, what you accept now will normally need to be guided, implicitly or explicitly, by the premisses or inference-rules that you have accepted previously. So in such cases you will be deliberately schooling your present thoughts to fit such premisses or rules, and you will evaluate your hypotheses as correct or incorrect, probable or improbable, in accordance with those criteria. The judgement that a clinician makes now on the prospects of his patient's recovery might be one that consciously or unconsciously obeys criteria which he accepted long ago when he was a student. But, when one belief is said to give rise to another, the outcome is conceived of as being involuntary rather than a manifestation of obedience to principle. Once you come to believe that the driver ahead has lost control, you can't help yourself believing that his car will crash. In short, though acceptances *may* be arbitrary or irrational, they are normally predicted or explained as outcomes of reasoning in conformity with rules, whereas beliefs are predicted or explained as resulting from the operations of relevant causal factors, such as sensory stimuli or the transmission of information.

We may conclude, therefore, strictly speaking, that people are held responsible and accountable for what they accept or fail to accept, not for what they believe or fail to believe. For example, a person may be culpable for not accepting the obvious, but not for not believing it. Again, a modern juror is culpable for relying on beliefs that he has acquired from what he has heard about the defendant outside the court and adopting those beliefs as premisses on which to base conclusions about the defendant's guilt or innocence. But he is not culpable for having the beliefs, if he could not help hearing what he did. People are also often at fault for not acquainting themselves with relevant facts or for not acquiring relevant mental disciplines, since these are voluntary processes that may cause appropriate beliefs to arise. But people are hardly to be blamed (though they may be subjects for pity, contempt, admira-

---

[23] Recognition of others' pretences may come later still: see A. M. Leslie, 'Pretence, Autism and the Basis of "Theory of Mind"', *The Psychologist*, 13 (1990), pp. 120–2.

tion, or wonder) if they still lack the belief that p even after acquainting themselves with evidence, or acquiring mental disciplines, that are normally adequate to produce it. And that covers the case of the Victorian wife who thinks that she has a moral obligation to believe that her husband is impeccably virtuous. On the other hand, if the known evidence that p is quite adequate, then, even if a person himself lacks any feeling of conviction that p, he is rightly held responsible for not accepting that p. If there is well-publicized medical evidence that a certain kind of vaccination is beneficial for a child's health, then the parents who know of that evidence are responsible for not drawing the appropriate conclusions. In such cases it is justifiable to be less tolerant of others' being misguided in what they accept than of their being mistaken in what they believe. Of course, a person is not necessarily to be blamed for every mistake in what he accepts. He may, for example, have been cunningly deceived by someone whom he had good reason to trust. But at least we can in principle question whether he, or someone else, should be blamed for the mistake, whereas no such question arises about his mistaken beliefs (as distinct from any negligence or deception that may have led to those beliefs). A person can be in a position to accept that p, even though, as Wittgenstein[24] saw, we can't say that he is in a position to believe that p.

This point about culpability applies not only to people's attitudes towards factual propositions but also to their attitudes towards normative ones. Thus we tend to be somewhat less censorious in relation to people who have moral beliefs with which we disagree than we are in relation to those who deliberately accept rules of conduct that we find objectionable. In the former kind of case allowances are commonly made for the involuntariness with which people's consciences operate, or for the pressures of indoctrination to which they succumbed in childhood. But if we are concerned only with the deliberate acceptance of objectionable rules of conduct we normally assume that people deserve to suffer the consequences of their decisions. In a country at war, it would seem more reasonable to tolerate conscientious objectors than to tolerate those who argue just that they signed a pledge to refuse military service.

[24] L. Wittgenstein, *On Certainty* (Oxford: Blackwell, 1969), para. 556.

Indeed, there are often good reasons for accepting that *p* which are not good reasons for believing that *p*, whereas good reasons for believing that *p* which are not also good reasons for accepting that *p* are rather rare. Thus no ethical or prudential reasons for accepting that *p* can be said—*stricto sensu*—to be reasons for believing that *p*, since ethics and prudence are concerned only with what is in our power or under our control. For example, the rules of professional practice may be a good reason for a lawyer's accepting, in the context of a particular trial, that his client is innocent, and for pleading accordingly, though those rules are not a good reason for him to believe this. But we have to ponder on the rather abnormal situation of someone's swearing that he will never use some confidentially imparted piece of information as a premiss, in order to think up an example of a person's having a good reason to believe that *p* without any good reason to accept that *p*.

Perhaps it will be objected that the conception of occurrent belief as a feeling, and the consequential treatment of belief-dispositions as involuntary, are incompatible with the fact that we can speak of reasons for believing that *p*, of the rationality of this belief, of the justification for it, of what people ought to believe, and so on. Of course—the objector will admit—there is a sense in which the phrase 'reason for' functions as a synonym for the phrase 'cause of', as when geologists talk about the reasons for earthquakes. In that sense we can speak of the causes of a belief as the reasons for it, and the existence of a reason for a belief is not incompatible with the conception of that belief as an involuntary disposition to have certain feelings. 'The reason for his believing that Rabbitslice is the best cat-food', we may be told, 'is the subliminal advertising to which he has been subjected.' But, in addition to that type of retrospective point of view, from which we can discuss the reasons for (alias causes of) an already established belief, there is also a prospective point of view from which we can ask such questions as: What should I believe about *x*? Am I to believe that *p*? What reasons are there to believe that *p*? Is it rational to believe that *p*? And so on. From this latter point of view—the objector will insist—the issue is still open, alternative outcomes are conceivable, 'reason for' cannot be synonymous with 'cause of', and the relation between the reasons and the belief is normative or justificatory rather than causal or genetic. Moreover, if 'reason for' can have such a sense in the prospective context, it must also be able to have it sometimes in the retrospective one, since a person can easily move without equivocation from speaking of the reasons that would justify his belief that p, if he came to have this belief, to speaking of the same reasons as justifying his recently acquired belief that p. And, if he then comes to speak of these as the reasons for his belief, his remark may well be echoed by others though not in the sense in which 'reason for' is synonymous with 'cause of'. Accordingly—the objection runs—we should look on belief not as an involuntary, uncontrollable disposition to have certain feelings, but as a mental act that is open to a reasoned choice between alternatives.

But the trouble with this objection is that by parity of reasoning jealousy, alarm, despondency, and joy too should be mental acts and not involuntary feeling-dispositions. For we can ask such questions as: Should I be jealous of George? What reasons are there for you to be jealous of Paul? Is his jealousy of Tom irrational? And so too, *mutatis mutandis*, with alarm, despondency, joy, etc. Yet these certainly are involuntary feeling-dispositions, not mental acts. We may or may not be able to control their overt manifestations or the situations that produce them. But the feeling-dispositions themselves are certainly states of mind that we cannot switch on and off at will. Hence it is clear that in some circumstances a mental state can include an involuntary disposition to have mental feelings, such as jealousy, alarm, despondency, or joy, even though questions may arise about whether a disposition to have those particular feelings is, or would be, justified in the circumstances in question. Indeed, if the reason for George's anger is that he will not be at the party tonight, what is called a 'reason' here cannot strictly be called a 'cause' because it lies in the future.

In other words, there is an important sector of our mental life on which we impose inter-personally accepted standards of rationality and justifiability despite the fact that it is not under our direct control. No doubt this is connected with the fact that we are at least in principle able to exercise various kinds of *in*direct influence on the dispositions to have such feelings. We can try to induce or inhibit our dispositions to have feelings of belief, jealousy, alarm, etc. that p by acquainting ourselves with all the relevant evidence and evaluating it within a balanced perspective, by discussing the problem with our friends, or maybe by prayer, meditation, exercise, or deep breathing. But that does not make our feeling-dispositions, whatever they may turn out in the end to be, any less involuntary when they actually arise.

§5. THE DEDUCTIVE CLOSURE ISSUE

It is tempting to say that, while the explicit, direct act of acceptance involves a conscious adoption of a policy about premisses or rules of inference, a person also accepts indirectly or unconsciously all the deductive consequences of each of the propositions that he accepts explicitly, and of any of their conjunctions, whether or not he is himself aware of those consequences or able or disposed to work them out. That would be because, when the conjunction p_1 & p_2 & ... & p_n entails q and a person decides to adopt the policy of taking p_1, p_2 ... and p_n as premisses, or rules, he seems to stay effectively on course by taking q as a premiss, inasmuch as anything that is part of the content of q will also be part of the content of p_1 & p_2 & ... & p_n. Or, in other words, if he adopts p as a foundation for his inferences he seems to commit himself to regarding any deductive consequence of p as such a foundation also. So, if a person announces to others that he has accepted certain propositions, he seems to imply acceptance also of their necessary consequences or equivalents, and thus to create a presumption about how he will think and act so far as he knows those consequences. Also, if he says that everyone ought to accept p_1, p_2 ... and p_n, he implies that everyone ought to accept all the deductive consequences of those propositions too. So, even if he does not announce to others his decision to accept that p, this decision certainly seems, at least on first consideration, to reach indefinitely far (unless he changes his mind) beyond any consequences or equivalents that he may perceive at the moment. Correspondingly, his implied or indirect acceptance of a proposition would be either intentional, if it derived wholly from perceived implications, or unintentional if it derived otherwise.

But, although it is tempting to analyse acceptance in this way, there is a serious difficulty that the analysis encounters. If acceptance is thus closed under the relationship of deducibility, then a good deal of what a person may accept is either controversial or perhaps even unknown. A good deal of it is certainly controversial, because of the competing theories that exist about deducibility. For example, which side is to be taken in regard to the so-called paradoxes of strict implication?[25] Do you accept every necessary truth if you accept even one proposition, and do you accept every proposition if you accept an inconsistent set of premisses? And a good deal of what you accept may even be unknown, if there is still some progress to be made in the logic or mathematics of deducibility. For example, it was not until 1752 that Clairaut proved that the correct values for the forward movement of the apse of the moon could be deduced from the axioms of Newtonian mechanics. So it seems odd to claim that even before then anyone who accepted those axioms thereby accepted the relevant equations of lunar movement, whether or not he was aware of the latter. At any rate Clairaut's proof was treated at the time as being itself a prize-winning new item of knowledge rather than as something that had already been accepted with the acceptance of the mathematical principles on which it depended.[26] It was an item for acceptance on its own merits. Indeed, if people thought otherwise about such matters, there would be no new theorems accepted in any existing branch of logic or mathematics, because every theorem would have been already accepted—unconsciously—when the postulates from which it has now been proved were accepted. It would be as if every logician or mathematician were implicitly credited with omniscience.

In order to avoid these paradoxes we need to distinguish between objective and subjective closure under deducibility. Acceptance is *objectively* closed under deducibility if and only if necessarily, for any p_1, p_2 ... and p_n and for any q that is deducible from the conjunction of p_1, p_2 ... and p_n, anyone who accepts p_1, p_2 ... and p_n, accepts q. Acceptance is *subjectively* closed under deducibility if and only if necessarily for any p_1, p_2 ... and p_n and for any

---

[25] See C. I. Lewis and C. H. Langford, *Symbolic Logic* (New York: Dover Publications, 1959), p. 174. I shall prescind here from discussing the formal structure of reasoning about revisions in what we believe or accept. But it is to be noted that such discussions, frequent as they have been, are arguably premature, and risk confusion, in a context in which the fundamental distinction between belief and acceptance has yet to be clarified. See, for example, the treatment of the issue in S. O. Hansson, *Belief Base Dynamics* (Uppsala: Uppsala University, 1991), 46–50.

[26] See the remarks by Florian Cajori in the appendix to his edition of Newton's *Principia Mathematica* (Berkeley: University of California Press, 1962), pp. 648 ff.

q, anyone who accepts both the conjunction of p_1, p_2 ... and p_n and the deducibility of q from that conjunction, also accepts q. So far what has been supposed is that acceptance is objectively closed under deducibility, and it is this view that runs into the difficulty described. Specifically, a good deal of what a person accepts turns out to be either controversial or perhaps even unknown to him. But these paradoxes are avoided altogether if acceptance is instead regarded as merely being subjectively closed under deducibility. Your acceptance then reaches no further than the rule of *modus ponendo ponens* will carry you. If you accept both p and the deducibility of q from p, then you at least unintentionally, if not in fact intentionally, accept q. Of course, where q is deducible from p and you accept p, you *ought* always to accept q. But whether you *actually* do so or not depends on whether you also accept that q is deducible from p.

Why then is there a temptation to suppose that acceptance is objectively closed under deducibility? Perhaps the explanation is that it is easy to have an unnoticed inclination to treat acceptance as a speech-act rather than as the adoption of a mental policy. Anyone who declares to his hearers that he accepts that p gives them a warrant to suppose that he is committing himself to at least the commonly agreed logical consequences of that proposition. He cannot excuse himself later by saying that he himself was not aware of the rules determining those consequences. And there would be something rather odd in his saying 'I accept that p but I don't accept all the consequences of that proposition.' But, where acceptance is a tacit mental decision, the speaker and the hearer are the same person, as it were, and the commitment therefore extends no further than the speaker's own inferential ability can discern its consequences. So there is nothing odd in saying, 'He accepts that p but doesn't accept all the consequences of that proposition.' It is also easy to confuse what a person implies himself to accept with what he implicitly accepts. What you implicitly accept depends just on what is deducible from what you accept. But what you imply yourself to accept depends partly on what you declare yourself to accept.

Of course, there is also a sense of 'accept' in which the set of propositions—whether factual or normative—that is said to be accepted by a particular person is not thereby implied to possess even the subjective form of deductive closure. In that sense a person may be said to accept that p only so far as he *explicitly* adopts the policy of taking the proposition that p as a premiss. Such an attribution of acceptance imputes direct acknowledgement of what is accepted and says nothing about the accepter's relationship to other propositions. But it would be a mistake to think that acceptance in that sense of the term is a different kind of mental act or attitude from acceptance in the sense in which it is deductively closed. What is different lies just in how much is said about the act or attitude, not in how much there is to be said. If you explicitly adopt the policy of taking $p_1, p_2 \ldots$ and p_n as available premisses, where you also accept that these propositions entail q, you are in any case implicitly committed to thereby so taking q. This element of implicit commitment provides a basis for subjective deductive closure that is partially analogous to the way in which the utterance of a promise provides a basis for imputing, *ceteris paribus*, consequential obligations. If George promises to pay Peter £500 in cash at 9 a.m. next Friday, then—his circumstances being what they are—George thereby implicitly commits himself to getting the money out of his bank account some time earlier, even if he did not have this implicit commitment in mind at the time at which he made his explicit commitment or promise. And similarly, if George now decides to accept that p, in the sense of taking the proposition that p as a premiss wherever it is relevant to do so, George now implicitly commits himself (by his own decision) to taking as a premiss any proposition that he accepts to be a consequence of p, unless or until he changes his mind. Admittedly, at the time George took his decision he may have failed to bear in mind very many consequences of p that he accepted to be such. But that does not let George off the hook of acceptance in regard to any propositions that he accepted to be consequences, any more than failure to attend to the obvious consequences of his promise would exempt him from the corresponding commitment to get the money out of his bank. After all, if George decides to accept that p, he decides on the policy of going along with p as a premiss whatever he may see the consequences of p to be. Hence, in regard to any proposition q that he indeed accepts to be a consequence of p, he has effectively, even if not knowingly, also decided to go along with the availability of q for use as a premiss, since p underwrites any such use of q. George's implicit commitment is necessarily, albeit unwittingly, embraced within his explicit one.

Certainly, any reason that a person has for accepting that p is actually held to be also, if p is accepted to entail q, a reason for accepting that q. So we might just as well adopt a sense of 'accept' that reflects this. Someone may object here that, if he accepts that he should light a firework's fuse and then step back, he does not thereby accept that he should just light a firework's fuse, since the former course of action is quite safe while the latter may not be and the acceptance of unsafe advice can hardly be implicit in the acceptance of safe advice. But what is unsafe is to accept that one should light the firework's fuse and then *not* step back, and this is patently not implicit in accepting that one should light the fuse and then step back. If the conjunction of p and q is accepted to entail q, a policy of taking p & q as a premiss certainly entails or embraces a policy of taking q as a premiss. The latter policy is implicit in the former. But it does not follow that, if it is prudent to pursue the former policy on its own, so too it is prudent to pursue the latter on its own. Similarly it does not follow that, if a person accepts that he should post a letter, he thereby accepts that he should either post or burn it. What he has accepted is an instruction that, if executed, will make it false that he neither posts the letter nor burns it.

Acceptance, then, is to be regarded as subjectively closed under deducibility. How about belief? The fact is that you are not intellectually pledged by a set of *beliefs*, however strong, to each deductive consequence of that set of beliefs, even if you recognize it to be such. That is because belief that p is a disposition to feel that p, and feelings that arise in you, or grow on you, or come over you, through involuntary processes of which you may be wholly or partly unconscious, no more impose their logical consequences on you than do the electoral campaign posters that people stick on your walls without your consent. Beliefs carry no commitments. They are neither intentional nor unintentional. So the statement that you believe that p does not necessarily imply that you believe that q, even where q is quite a close and well-recognized logical, conceptual, or mathematical consequence of p. If your logical, conceptual, or mathematical perception is rather limited, inactive, incoherent, or uninfluential, you may well feel it true that p and that if p then q, without feeling it true that q. You will just be failing to put two and two together, as it were. And detective-story writers, for example, show us how often and easily we can fail to do this with our beliefs. Admittedly, if you do not believe the immediate and obvious consequences of the proposition that p, this may be treated as evidence that you do not really believe p at all. If you believe that p_1 and that p_2, you are as a matter of contingent fact normally expected to believe their immediate and obvious consequences, because you are presumed to exercise sufficient logical, conceptual, or mathematical perceptiveness in this respect. The one belief is expected to cause the others, as it normally does. But it may well not do so on particular occasions.

Of course, if you believe that p, you may be said to have an *implicit* belief that q. But a purely implicit belief that q is no more a kind of belief that q than a toy soldier is a kind of soldier. A purely implicit belief carries with it no disposition to have appropriate feelings (whereas implicit acceptance is a kind of acceptance because of the commitment carried with it).

This difference between belief and acceptance is easy to miss because anyone's proclaiming that *he* believes that p certainly does normally commit him to accepting any propositions that he accepts to be logical consequences of the proposition that p. But that commitment stems just from a fact about the speech-act of proclaiming 'I believe that p' with an emphasis on the word 'I' rather than on the word 'believe'. By making this affirmative first-person present indicative proclamation one commonly expresses acquiescence in, or content with, one's own belief and thereby affirms one's acceptance that p, or at least one's opinion that the proposition that p deserves acceptance. Utterances in the second or third person, or in the first person with 'believe' emphasized, or in the past tense, may be contrasted here. 'John believes that p' does not impute acceptance. Note too how utterance of 'I feel that p' may suggest a certain tentativeness in the feeler. But it does not follow that non-tentative beliefs are therefore not to be regarded as feelings at all, since utterances of 'He feels that p' or 'I felt that p' (or even of '*I* feel that p', where the feeler, not the feeling, is emphasized) do not normally convey the same suggestion.

In sum, subjective deductive closure is not implicit in all propositions about a person's beliefs in the way that it is implicit in all propositions about what he accepts. Writers on the logic of belief who treat belief even as subjectively—let alone objectively—closed under deducibility are either confusing, or at least confounding, belief with acceptance. And perhaps it is worth pointing out too that even acceptance is subject to certain restrictions in this connection. Though acceptance that p involves a policy of treating this proposition as a premiss for one's inductive as well as for one's deductive reasoning, it does not follow that, if you accept that p_1, p_2 ... and p_n and that these premisses provide some positive inductive support for the hypothesis that q (while none of your accepted premisses count as inductive evidence against the hypothesis that q), then you must also accept that q. This is partly because quite a high level of inductive support may need to be derivable from your premisses if it is to be justifiable to accept that q. But it also has to be borne in mind that (especially where there are competing hypotheses) even a high level of evidential support may not suffice to justify acceptance that q, because other factors besides evidence—factors such as relative simplicity or fruitfulness—may be relevant to the question whether q or some rival hypothesis should be accepted.

§6. SOME OTHER LOGICAL ISSUES

Just as belief and acceptance differ from one another in regard to deductive closure, so too they differ in regard to the demand for consistency.

Consider belief first. If belief that p involves the disposition to feel it true that p, then you cannot be said to believe that, literally, both p and not-p: such a feeling has no intelligible content. What about belief that p and belief that not-p? These do at least involve separately intelligible feelings. But are such a pair of beliefs combinable?

It can hardly be denied that people sometimes oscillate wildly, and even very rapidly, between belief and disbelief. They may feel that different arguments or different pieces of evidence are tugging them in different directions. They may have different feelings on the matter in different contexts or locations.

But you may be tempted to deny the possibility of simultaneously believing both that p and that not-p, because you presume that, for any p and q, the combination of belief that p with belief that q entails belief that p and q. Since it follows from this presumption that belief that p and belief that not-p entails belief that p and not-p, you are tempted to conclude, because belief that p and not-p is impossible, that it is also impossible simultaneously to believe both that p and that not-p. But if, as argued above (in §5), belief is not closed under deducibility, you have no warrant to infer that belief that p and belief that q combine to entail belief that p and q. So there is no reason here to deny that belief that p and belief that not-p, when suitably weak, hesitant, or faltering, may sometimes be combinable, either by the actual coexistence of opposed feelings or at least by the coexistence of opposing dispositions. If a person has only a weak feeling that it is true that p, he may not be wholly resistant to also having a weak feeling that not-p, especially where there are powerful conflicting arguments, or where there is only a little evidence, with some of it in the one direction and some in the other. That is why it makes sense to say such things as 'He half-believes that p and half-believes that not-p'. Or, if he has a hesitant or faltering belief that p, he may also have a similarly infirm belief that not-p. His cognitive or evaluative dispositions are then in a turmoil of conflict with one another, which we may describe by saying, 'He has some inclination to believe that p and some that not-p', or even, 'He is in two minds about whether it is true that p.'

We do not even have to suppose weakness of belief, however, when we consider whether the belief that p is in principle combinable with the belief that q if q is not itself the negation of p but merely implies that negation. In such a case, since belief is not deductively closed, belief that q will not entail belief that not-p and, especially if he does not notice the fact that q implies not-p, a man may easily be supposed both to believe that p and to believe that q—albeit that his belief that q is not as clear-cut as it would be if he were aware that q implies not-p. It is just a contingent matter, therefore, whether a person is capable of combining belief that p with belief that q in this kind of case.

The element of contingency is even more marked when we consider whether a person can be said to be capable of believing each of a set of three or more propositions where it is logically, conceptually, or mathematically impossible for all the propositions to be true. For example, it does seem that he might be said to believe quite strongly that he ought to do x, that he ought to do y, and that it is in practice impossible for him to do both. And, as the inconsistency of the propositions becomes less glaring and explicit, it becomes even easier to suppose that someone believes them all.

For example, there is nothing odd about the description of someone both as believing each of p_1, p_2 ... and p_n and also as believing the conjunction p_1 & p_2 ... & p_n to be false, where n is rather large, since he may well believe that somewhere or other among his beliefs—he doesn't know where—at least one error may be present. Notoriously that is how the author of a book, if sufficiently modest, might describe himself in the preface. Indeed, so far from its being unreasonable for a person to feel that he may have at least one mistaken belief, it may well be unreasonable for him to feel that he has not got at least one mistaken belief. He must have come across some of the widespread evidence in favour of the generalization that everyone is, at least occasionally, led into errors of belief by his own misunderstandings, muddled associations, wishful thinking, carelessness, unperceptiveness, or mental or physical laziness, or by the mistakes or deceits of others.

On these issues we now need to compare acceptance, point by point, with belief. And here, because acceptance, in contrast with belief, is voluntary, we have to consider not only what the *concept* of acceptance permits but also what our standards of rationality require. The domain of what we are in principle able to accept is a good deal more extensive than the domain of what it is intellectually right and proper to accept, just as the domain of voluntary action is a good deal more extensive than the domain of what it is morally right or practically prudent to do. So even a starkly self-contradictory proposition (of the form: p and not-p) is in principle available for acceptance, though acceptance of it would arguably be irrational since in classical logic every proposition whatever would be deducible from it. Similarly it is conceptually possible for a person to be said to accept both that p and that not-p—even in the same context and over the same period. People who accept both that p and that not-p might appear annoyingly inconsistent or paralysingly unselective and indecisive. But perhaps they do occasionally exist, however irrational they may rightly be condemned as being. After all, who except a classical logician accepts that every proposition whatever is deducible from a contradiction? *A fortiori* it is also conceptually possible for a person to accept each of a set of two or more propositions that are collectively inconsistent. Indeed in some cases the inconsistency may even be difficult to detect, or at least not obvious to the inexpert logician or mathematician. And, if a *reductio ad absurdum* proof in any case requires us temporarily to assume the truth of each of what is in fact an inconsistent set of propositions, it could hardly be *impossible* for someone—perhaps ignorant of the proof—actually to accept every member of such a set. But it is, of course, just as *irrational* to accept this set as to accept a pair of obviously inconsistent propositions, like p and not-p. And here there is an important difference between belief and acceptance. Because belief is not deductively closed it is not necessarily an intellectual disaster if a person does have an inconsistency between some of his beliefs. But for acceptance the analogous situation may be disastrous. Since acceptance is—subjectively—deductively closed, and everybody accepts that any two premises combine to entail their conjunction, it follows that accepting that p and accepting that not-p will commit a person to accepting that p and not-p, which is certainly irrational. There is thus a good reason for not accepting each of p_1, p_2 . . . and p_n and also the negation of the conjunction p_1 & p_2 & . . . & p_n. The author of a book should not, in his preface, be as modest about errors of acceptance as he may be about errors of belief. Acceptance is inherently motivated towards the elimination of inconsistency.

It should be noticed, however, that belief and acceptance do resemble one another in respect of certain other logical properties. In particular, they both lack any necessary implications about iteration.

If a person believes that p, he may or may not be disposed to reflect on what he is doing. So he may or may not also be disposed to feel it true that he is disposed to feel it true that p—he may or may not believe that he believes that p. Indeed, even an occurrent state of belief may not be accompanied by an occurrent state of awareness that it is occurring. Few people are so introspective that, whenever they feel it true that p, they also feel it true that they feel it true that p. That is why it is wrong to hold, as Davidson does,[27] that a person cannot have a belief unless he understands the possibility of being mistaken and therefore of having a false belief. When you believe that a coin is genuinely gold, you must understand the logical possibility of its not being gold—that is, you must be aware of what it would be like for the coin not to be gold.

[27] D. Davidson, *Inquiries into Truth and Interpretation* (Oxford: Clarendon Press, 1984), p. 170.

Equally when you believe iteratedly that you have a true (first-order) belief that p you must understand the logical possibility that you do not have such a true (first-order) belief. But you don't have to understand something like this if your belief is not an iterated (second-order) one. That is why an animal may be ascribed a belief without being ascribed the concept of belief. When it believes that p, it does not also believe that it believes that p.

It may be tempting to argue that, since having an occurrent feeling that p entails consciously believing that p, while consciously believing that p involves being conscious that one is believing that p, therefore feeling that p entails feeling that one is feeling that p. But this argument has a false premiss. To believe consciously that p no more entails being conscious that one is believing that p, than being consciously, as distinct from subconsciously, motivated by a sexual urge entails being introspectively conscious that one is so motivated.

Similarly, if a person accepts that p, he may or may not accept that he accepts that p. For example, a person may in fact long since have decided to go along with certain premisses about the virtue of doing one's duty to one's children even in the most trying circumstances while, perhaps for reasons of moral humility or from fear of backsliding, he resists taking it as a premiss that he accepts those ethical propositions. He is certainly not committed, by his policy of taking the proposition that p as a premiss, to the policy of taking it as a premiss that he does take p as a premiss. For on different kinds of issue people may set different standards of self-knowledge as their objective.

Also, believing that you believe that p doesn't entail that you do believe that p, since you might believe that you were disposed to feel something on appropriate occasions and then find, when it came to the point, that the feeling didn't actually emerge. And accepting that you accept that p doesn't entail that you accept that p, since you might have practical reasons—to sleep easy at night, say—for accepting that you accept that p, and yet have good evidential reasons for not accepting that p.

Again, when considered outside relevant context, sentences predicating acceptance that p resemble sentences predicating belief that p in being open to both *de dicto* and *de re* interpretations. Consequently, that much-discussed type of ambiguity need not concern us here at all. For example, the sentence,

George accepts that the bank-manager is a spy

may either (in its *de dicto* interpretation) report every particular of George's thought as it actually went through his mind. Or (in its *de re* interpretation) it may report a thought of George's that happens to be about the bank-manager, whether or not George accepts that it is, since, though Ralph happens to be the bank-manager, what actually went through George's mind was only the thought that Ralph is a spy.

Moreover, the difference between belief and acceptance does not affect difficulties about the substitutivity of identically referring expressions. That is to say, preservation of truth-value is not guaranteed when any such substitution takes place in *de dicto* contexts whether of belief or of acceptance. But the reason why this is so is different in the two cases, and the difference needs to be remarked. So far as belief is concerned, a person's credal feelings are naturally liable to vary not only with the real-world issue on which they are focused but also with the details of that issue's representation in his mind. What feelings he is disposed to have may well be causally influenced by how the issue presents itself to him. But, so far as acceptance is concerned, the consideration that protects its content from the inter-substitutability of identically referring expressions is quite a different one. Here it is the limited eligibility of the content for use as a premiss that imposes a strict limit, in linguistic terms, on what we may take as being accepted, since this limited eligibility is crucial to acceptance. Any identity of reference that is relevant, but not recognized by the accepter as being already implicit, must be made the content of an additional premiss about what he accepts, if it is to legitimate substitution.

Nor is the difference between belief and acceptance relevant to the controversy between what are called 'internalist' and 'externalist' theories of content.[28] The question at issue in the controversy is whether, in order to identify the content of a mental attitude with accuracy, one may need to look not only at features of the person who has the attitude but also at features of the entity that is the subject of this attitude. Or, in other words, could two people on different planets undergo the same sensory stimuli, exhibit the same neurological processes, and manifest the same behaviour, and

---

[28] See, for example, C. McGinn, *Mental Content* (Oxford: Blackwell, 1989), pp. 1–119.

yet have different beliefs, desires, etc.—for example, because the substance on which their attention was concentrated had different chemical structures on the two planets? Externalists answer 'yes' to this question, internalists answer 'no'. But whatever the correct resolution of the controversy the same answer must apply both to belief and to acceptance, because it must be in principle possible to move from one to the other without change of content. People often accept just what they believe, and believe just what they accept.

II
Purposive Explanation

It is commonly said (§7) that folk-psychological explanations of human behaviour proceed by citing relevant combinations of beliefs and desires. But (§8) in fact they often cite instead relevant combinations of what the agent accepts as his premises and what he adopts as his goals. Recognition of this (§9) helps to clarify the limited extent to which infants and animals may be attributed purposes. Their position is complementary (§10) to that of human organizations and programmed artefacts. These points bear (§11) not only on the retrospective explanation of human behaviour but also on prospective reasoning in prediction, persuasion, or deliberation. And (§12) various issues raised by the question 'Are reasons causes?' can now be clarified.

§7. THE INVOLUNTARINESS OF BELIEF AND DESIRE

It is a widely held thesis in contemporary philosophy that in their everyday explanations of one another's actions people normally cite the beliefs and desires of the agent.[1] These are the main explanations that folk psychology is said to propose. According to Fodor, for example, 'we have no idea of how to explain ourselves to ourselves except in a vocabulary which is *saturated* with belief/

[1] J. A. Fodor, *Psychosemantics: The Problem of Meaning in the Philosophy of Mind* (Cambridge, Mass.: MIT Press, 1987), pp. 1–26; I. Scheffler, *The Anatomy of Inquiry* (New York: Knopf, 1963), pp. 88–110; C. Peacocke, *Holistic Explanation: Action, Space, Interpretation* (Oxford: Clarendon Press, 1979), pp. 3 ff.; A. Morton, *Frames of Mind* (Oxford: Clarendon Press, 1980), p. 72; D. Davidson, *Essays on Actions and Events* (Oxford: Clarendon Press, 1982), pp. 3–4; S. P. Stich, *From Folk Psychology to Cognitive Science: The Case against Belief* (Cambridge, Mass.: MIT Press, 1983), p. 217; G. Strawson, *Freedom and Belief* (Oxford: Clarendon Press, 1986), p. 34; P. Churchland, 'Folk Psychology and the Explanation of Human Behaviour', *Proceedings of the Aristotelian Society*, Supp. vol. 62 (1988), p. 212; A. Clark, *Microcognition: Philosophy, Cognitive Science and Parallel Distributed Processing* (Cambridge, Mass.: MIT Press, 1989), p. 5; J. Bennett, 'Why is Belief Involuntary?', *Analysis*, 50 (1990), p. 97.

desire psychology'. Numerous other mental states and attitudes are also mentioned as capable of taking the place of beliefs and desires in some such explanations. But amid this broad-minded pluralism beliefs and desires still dominate the scene, and the crucial difference between beliefs and belief-like attitudes, on the one side, and acceptance and acceptance-like attitudes, on the other, tends to remain unnoticed. Dennett, for example, considers it important to distinguish between beliefs and opinions (pp. 15–16 above), but has nothing to say about explanation in terms of opinions and desires, as distinct from explanation in terms of beliefs and desires.[2] I want to concentrate attention in the present chapter, therefore, on the implications of the distinction between belief and acceptance for the analysis of purposive explanation, even if in so doing I have to ignore numerous other distinctions that would have to be drawn in a more comprehensive treatment.

Four fairly obvious points need to be made at the outset, because someone who gives a purposive explanation of an action in terms of the agent's belief and desire does not normally intend that why, say, James did act *A* should be explained causally *just* by reference to the fact that James desired *B* and believed that doing *A* would bring about *B*. This simplistic model overlooks at least four relevant possibilities[3] that would have to be kept in mind if there is to be a full explanation, where the *explanans* cites a causally sufficient condition for the *explanandum* to occur. First, James might conceivably have been prevented from doing act *A*. So a full explanation has to include a mention of the fact that he was not prevented from doing this. Secondly, James might have made the bodily movements constituting act *A* without any credal attitude's being operative—as a result, perhaps, of some nervous reflex or of a compulsive urge. So a full explanation has to exclude this possibility. Conversely, to say that James's belief and desire combined to cause his action is to exclude any explanation in terms of nervous reflexes or compulsive urges. Thirdly, James might have had more than one relevant motive. He might in fact have shot George in order to kill his wife's lover, say, even though he also

---

[2] Compare D. Dennett, *Brainstorms: Philosophical Essays on Mind and Psychology* (Hassocks: Harvester Press, 1979), pp. 300–9, with D. Dennett, *The Intentional Stance* (Cambridge: MIT Press, 1983), pp. 13–35, 43–68, etc.

[3] See L. J. Cohen, 'Teleological Explanation', *Proceedings of the Aristotelian Society*, 51 (1951), pp. 255–92.

desired there to be a vacancy declared on the parish council and believed that shooting George would cause such a vacancy to be declared. So the dominant purpose of the act is given better by saying that at the time at which he did it James desired *B* more than anything else he believed doing *A* would bring about. Fourthly, by no means all the beliefs in such explanations are beliefs about one thing's causing another. For example, James might have visited Burford in order to visit the nearest Cotswold village. His relevant belief would then have been just that Burford is the nearest Cotswold village. Or, in order not to commit a sin, he might have refrained from shooting George. And his relevant belief would then have been just that shooting George would be a sin.

However, whether or not these points (and perhaps other similar ones) are recognized as widely as they should be, there is no doubt that explanations in terms of beliefs and desires are commonly thought to be widespread in ordinary people's attempts to understand one another. Indeed this type of purposive explanation is often said to constitute a central feature of what is called 'folk psychology'—a body of culturally or genetically inherited doctrine that is supposed, somewhat implausibly, to constitute a primitive attempt to solve some of the problems that academic psychology sets out to solve.

Now consider what the distinction between belief and acceptance implies here. Clearly we have to recognize that in addition to purposive explanations involving belief there are also purposive explanations involving acceptance. If James at last accepts, though he at least as yet does not really believe, that George is his wife's lover, then his purpose in shooting George may be just the same as if he did believe it. The purpose is perhaps still to kill his wife's lover, just as it would be if James really believed, but did not accept—i.e. did not take it as a premiss—that George is his wife's lover. Nevertheless there is an important difference between the two cases. If James *accepts* George's guilt, he is responsible at least for what one might conveniently call the direct or immediate cognitive input into the mental state that issues in James's shooting George. Acceptances are at the will of the accepter, who is therefore eligible for whatever praise, blame, reward or punishment is on offer. James's friends might dispassionately commend his respect for the evidence even if they deplored the violence of his action. On the other hand, if James believes, but does not accept, George's guilt, he is not directly responsible for the cognitive input at least so far as that input is involuntary. The belief is then part of the action's cause, not a premiss from which its appropriateness is inferred. This might be the case perhaps if James discovered George *in flagrante delicto* and killed him on impulse—i.e. without premeditation.

If therefore James is implied not to be directly responsible for the cognitive input into the situation when his act is explained in terms of his belief and desire, any direct responsibility that he has for the act must apparently be traceable to what one might conveniently call the affective input into the situation. It must be traceable to his desire. But are desires available at will, any more than beliefs are?

Desires, it seems, arise in one slowly, grow on one steadily or come over one suddenly, much as beliefs do. Like beliefs they can be planted in one's mind by events or by other people, but not by oneself. They are dispositions to have certain feelable yearnings, cravings, wishes, likings, or hankerings. And, like beliefs, they may vary in strength or weakness.

Desire that p, however, is not entailed by a disposition to bring it about that p, any more than belief that p is entailed by a disposition to act in accordance with that belief (pp. 8–11). Indeed, your actions on appropriate occasions may or may not be caused by the beliefs and desires that the actions appear to suggest. It is always open to you to pretend that you have beliefs or desires which you do not have or that you do not have beliefs or desires which you do have. Desires are also dispositions that conceivably may be influenced, partly or wholly, by subconscious processes, much as beliefs may be, and they can themselves be either conscious or unconscious. But we cannot form a desire at will, any more than we can form a belief at will. Of course, a person may want (or desire) to have other desires than he does have, especially if his actual desires are perverse, say, or destructive. For example, he may desire not to have the desire to smoke. But, however hard you desire to have better desires, this second-order desire may fail to be satisfied, just as any other desire may fail to be satisfied. So desires seem just as much a passive feature of the mind as beliefs are, and to the extent that we are not responsible for our beliefs we are also not responsible for our desires.

It does not follow from this that we are not to be held responsible for *any* purposive act that is explicable in terms of beliefs and desires. For we are indirectly culpable, as remarked earlier (§4), in respect of those mistaken beliefs that we have through not acquainting ourselves with evidence with which we ought to have acquainted ourselves or through not acquiring mental disciplines that we ought to have acquired. We also deserve credit for those true beliefs that we acquire as a result of acquainting ourselves with relevant evidence or through labouring at relevant disciplines. Equally a person deserves credit for having the good desires that he has fostered in himself. And he is blameworthy for having those desires that he ought to have tried to prevent growing on him. He ought to have reflected on the conflict of those desires with other, less reprehensible ones, or warned himself about their probable consequences.

§8. THE VOLUNTARINESS OF ACCEPTANCE AND GOAL-ADOPTION

However, quite apart from doing things to mould one's desires, one can also decide to satisfy or resist those desires. Anybody who cannot do this is mentally abnormal and the victim of genuinely uncontrollable urges. In such a case the explanation of an act by reference to the agent's relevant beliefs, desires, and incapacity for self-control is an explanation by reference only to involuntary features of the agent's mental life, and a purposive explanation of *this* kind does deprive an act of its culpability. That is how psychopathic killers, who use weapons rationally and purposively in order to achieve their horrific desires, may nevertheless be thought devoid of responsibility for their acts.

So, in normal people, while desires are intrinsically about as passive and involuntary as beliefs, they do have counterpart pro-attitudes that are as active and voluntary as acceptances. Among such active and voluntary counterparts of desires are the mental attitudes that consist in having such-or-such goals, aims, ends, objectives, plans, intentions, or policies. Indeed, these are the very attitudes in virtue of which we indulge or suppress our desires at will, just as we select beliefs at will to be the accepted premises for our proofs, argumentations, inferences, and deliberations or reject them as unsuitable for the purpose. And we also sometimes voluntarily give up goals, abandon intentions, alter plans, or resign ourselves to *faits accomplis*, much as we sometimes change our minds about our premisses. We are, therefore, normally held responsible for our goals, etc., just as for the acceptance of certain premisses and the rejection of others.

Thus, just as we can believe something without accepting it or accept it without believing it, so too we can desire something without intending to achieve it or intend to achieve it without desiring it. For example, a person may desire to be a lot richer than he is, without ever adopting self-enrichment as the goal that governs his career. Or he may desire regular exercise and actually be governed in his behaviour by this desire, without ever adopting the goal or policy of taking regular exercise. Or out of duty to his family he may adopt the goal of reducing his weight by a medically recommended amount, without either already having, or being able to develop, any feeling of desire for the exercise by which he plans to achieve this.

Perhaps it will be said that goals which control desires are really just conflicting, but more powerful, desires. For example, you may desire to practise the bassoon in your garden, and you suppress this desire because you also desire to get on well with your neighbours. But there is a difference between suppressing a desire because you have a conflicting but more powerful desire and suppressing a desire because you have a conflicting goal. The conflicting goal can be discarded at will, whereas the conflicting desire cannot.

To have only desires, and no intentions, goals, plans, or policies, is to be a creature of impulse, like an infant or an animal. But to have only intentions, goals, plans, or policies, and no desires, is to be as cold-blooded and emotionless as a guided missile or a central bank. In a well-integrated personality goals largely coincide with desires, just as acceptance generally goes along with belief.

Again, adopting x as one's goal may sometimes cause or help to cause desire for x, as when entering for a competition—maybe quite light-heartedly—comes to generate a desire to win it. We may compare how acceptance tends to promote belief (p. 18). But adopting x as one's goal or policy is not a possible reason for desiring x, just as accepting that p is not a reason for believing that p. On the other hand, just as belief that p is a prima facie reason for accepting that p, so too having a desire for x is certainly one possible reason for adopting *x* as one's goal (though it may well not be the only, or the best reason, or even a sufficient one). This might be, for example, because there is just a presumption, which can be rebutted in appropriate circumstances, that the desire to *x* (for example, to eat more fruit) would not have arisen at all without its being favoured by at least some respectable considerations, such as bodily needs. And that presumption corresponds to the presumption, in the case of a certain belief, that it would not have arisen at all without there having been at least some data in its favour. Or perhaps instead someone may think that in the short lives permitted us we should gratify as many of our desires as we can manage to gratify without preventing others from gratifying theirs.

This analogy between the desire/goal-seeking distinction and the belief/acceptance one does have some important fractures. For example, acceptance can be regarded as a species of policy-adoption, whereas belief is hardly a species of desire. But the parallelism extends quite far. In particular it is clearly marked in regard to deductive closure. In so far as a person is said to adopt *x* as his goal, without any pertinent limitation, he is thereby implied to aim at doing whatever he accepts to be logically, mathematically, or conceptually necessary to achieve *x*, just as a person who accepts that *p* is thereby committed to accepting all the propositions that he accepts to be deductive consequences of the proposition that *p*. The former aims, intentionally or unintentionally, at doing whatever *x* is accepted to entail, just as the latter accepts whatever *p* is accepted to entail. Similarly, on the other hand, having a desire for *x* and a desire for *y* does not entail having a desire for *x* and *y*, just as a belief that *p* and a belief that *q* doesn't entail a belief that *p* and *q* (pp. 31–2). Though you may have a desire to empty a petrol tank now and you may also have a desire to light a cigarette now, you don't therefore have a desire to do both things now. But if you plan or intend to do each of them you thereby plan or intend to do both of them, and it is just as well that you should be aware of this.

Again, you may well have inconsistent desires. Perhaps you would like to be a grandparent one day but would not like to procreate any children of your own. And you may actually commit yourself to inconsistent goals or policies. For there is nothing logically inconsistent about describing someone as having both decided to aim at the achievement, and also decided to aim at the non-achievement, of a particular goal. But it would nevertheless be irrational so to aim (unless some further objective is advanced by combining the two policies).

At the time, admittedly, a person may not discern everything that it is logically necessary for him to adopt as a partial goal in order to achieve his overall goal, just as a person who accepts that *p* and that *q* may not discern all the necessary consequences to which this acceptance commits him. Goal adoption, like acceptance, may thus be unintentional in some cases even though intentional in others. But the situation is quite different with desires, as it is with beliefs. Like beliefs, desires are neither intentional nor unintentional. The states of mind that arise in you, or grow on you, or come over you, as beliefs and desires do, are not capable of imposing any consequential commitments on you. *A fortiori* they raise no issue about your further intentions. However strongly you desire *x*, you are no more committed thereby to desiring whatever you believe to be logically implicit in achieving *x* than your believing that *p* commits you to believing all the propositions that you believe to be deductive consequences of the proposition that *p*. Neither beliefs nor desires commit you to putting two and two together.

An analogous point can be made about the desire for *x* when you believe that bringing about *y* is *causally* necessary in order to achieve *x*. You are not committed by having this desire and belief to having also a desire for *y*. Indeed the undesirability, in your eyes, of bringing about *y* may be the very reason why you never satisfy your desire for *x*. But it is quite different with goals or policies. If your fixed goal is to achieve *x* and you firmly accept that bringing about *y* is causally necessary in order to achieve *x*, those who know these facts will attribute to you the implicit goal of bringing about *y*. Thus the doctrine that he who wills the end wills the means, as far as he thinks that he knows it, applies to the pursuit of goals or policies, not to the experiencing of desires. And just as what I said earlier about acceptance echoes a lot of what used to be said about what was often called 'judgement', so too what I am now saying about pursuing a goal, following a policy, or having an intention echoes a lot of what used to be said about what was called 'willing'. Indeed, without the possibility of such a distinction between goal-seeking and desire Kant's contrast between willing, on the one side, and the impulses and inclinations of sensibility, on the other, would be scarcely intelligible.[4]

Here too, as in the case of the distinction between belief and acceptance, the choice of vocabulary to mark the needed distinction is relatively unimportant. What is at issue is a conceivable difference in reality, not just a difference in idiom. For example, no doubt in practice people often declare their goal-adoptions by sentences that begin '*I* desire to . . . ', just as they often declare their acceptances by sentences that begin '*I* believe that . . . '. But the existence of the underlying differences is not in any way compromised by the looseness or flexibility of the vocabulary that is commonly used in these contexts.

Finally it should be noticed that acceptance is no less a basis for purposive explanation if the premisses concerned are adopted for non-evidential reasons—i.e. reasons that are ethical or prudential, etc. If on professional grounds a lawyer premisses that his client is innocent, then that is the premiss on which he should be expected to act and his adoption of that premiss will help to explain his subsequent behaviour.

The conclusion to which we are driven by all this is that purposive explanations of human action—of the kind that I have been considering—should be classifiable into at least four main categories. They perform their task by citing rationally interrelated beliefs and desires, beliefs and goals, acceptances and desires, or acceptances and goals. But what is believed may or may not coincide with what is accepted, and desires may or may not coincide with goals. So that an explanation belonging to one category may or may not need to go along with an explanation belonging to another category. Thus in perhaps the commonest kind of case the action to be explained not only stemmed from relevant beliefs and desires but was also done deliberately, with the agent deciding to achieve what he desired and also accepting what he believed about his means to that end. In another kind of case, however, an action may be explained in terms of relevant beliefs and desires alone, since it was done unthinkingly. If you brake suddenly in order to avoid hitting a child who has run into the road, you may have had no time at all to think consciously about

---

[4] I. Kant, *Fundamental Principles of the Metaphysics of Ethics*, trans. T. K. Abbott (London: Longmans, Green, 1907), p. 89.

the probable effect of your braking, though your action was none the less purposive and rational. Equally an action may be explained in terms of its author's deliberate purpose even if he lacked conviction about its probable effect. For example, if out of deference to your grandmother's experience in such matters, you accept that getting drunk regularly on tincture of nasturtium will cure your migraine, you may deliberately follow her advice even if you have no confidence that it is correct.

§9. THE PURPOSES OF ANIMALS, INFANTS, AND ADULTS

Despite the possibility of explanations in terms of acceptance and goal-adoption (as outlined in §8), explanation in terms of beliefs and desires is the pattern to which at least pride of place, and often exclusive attention, is given in most contemporary philosophical literature. It is what Dennett calls 'the intentional stance'.[5] Yet, considered on its own, it treats people rather like infants or animals are treated in everyday life. The actions to be explained are put down to the presence and causality of certain involuntary mental states—beliefs and desires—in a standard pattern of interconnection, which seems also to be the only pattern appropriate for the explanation of purposive behaviour in human infants or familiar mammals.

A pre-linguistic infant or a hungry domestic pet can hardly be said ever to be offered a reason for accepting that its meal is being prepared, because, lacking any linguistic formulations, it cannot be understood to adopt such a proposition as a premiss for deliberation or argumentation. In this sense it is not treated as capable of reasoning. But, on the evidence of its behaviour, it may well be attributed a belief, i.e. a disposition to feel, that its meal is being prepared. Similarly, though the infant or animal can hardly be supposed—without blatant anthropomorphism—to suspend judgement on the matter, its behaviour may well be construed as having been overwhelmed by doubt or uncertainty. And the cat that looks for mice every day in the same woodshed is more naturally said to have succumbed to the habit, than to have adopted the policy, of so doing. Such a creature is normally assumed in

[5] Dennett, *The Intentional Stance*, p. 17.

everyday life to lack the active mental attitudes, but to possess the passive ones along with some fairly coarse non-linguistic mechanism or model for representing—i.e. having in mind—states of affairs and successions of events. Indeed, most human adults do not take a pre-linguistic infant or domestic animal to have the self-consciousness, i.e. the awareness of its own identity over time, that it needs if it is to form goals or policies for its own future actions (even though it may have momentary intentions). Nor does such an animal seem to have the reasoning power that it needs if it is to construct plans for the achievement of goals or policies (unless perhaps certain primates have a modicum of this power). But no-one who associates familiarly with them ever denies that pre-linguistic infants and domestic mammals often have wants or desires for particular objects or events. The baby wants to drink the bottle of milk: the cat wants to eat the fish.

Of course, adult humans can have no warranty for making statements about the beliefs and desires of babies or cats if those statements are intended to receive a *de dicto* interpretation. We do not have any exact idea about what goes on in the minds of babies or cats or about how they achieve the representation of an object or event on which their beliefs or desires may be focused. But adult humans can and do legitimately try to describe the thoughts of babies or cats in *de re* terms. That is to say, adults can and do employ their own linguistic terminology of 'meal-preparation', 'bottle', 'milk', etc., in order to designate the events or objects that they assume to be at least partially known to babies or cats under some other mode of representation. And when they do this they need not impute to the babies' or cats' representations any syntactic or structural identity with their own linguistic representations.

Indeed it seems likely that failure to think in *de re* terms here is often what encourages philosophers to deny that an animal may be attributed beliefs and desires. They assume that such attributions are intended to be understood *de dicto*, and then rely on the strong and widely prevalent intuition that we cannot know exactly how an animal feels about the world, in order to persuade themselves that we are not entitled to make those attributions at all.

But if a baby or animal can in fact be attributed specific beliefs and desires—albeit in *de re* terms—we can hardly refuse to allow on occasion an interrelationship between its belief-state and desire-state that knits them together into a cause, the operation of which constitutes a form of purposive motivation. The dog fetches its lead in order to be taken for a walk, the cat watches the hole in the wall in order to ambush the mouse that it has heard, and so on. Consequently, if the purposive explanation of adult action were indeed confined to the analysis of beliefs and desires, as so many contemporary philosophers suggest, it would be no different in structure from the purposive explanation of infantile and animal behaviour.

Instead, it is just because human adults are held able to accept propositions as well as or instead of believing them, and to adopt goals as well as or instead of experiencing desires, that the type of purposefulness attributed to human adults is often radically different from that attributed to infants and animals. Some degree or degrees of voluntariness is then imputed to their explanatory mental states, the directness of responsibility with which they can be accredited is enhanced, and certain presumptive commitments may be inferred (in virtue of the fact that both acceptance and goal-adoption are subjectively closed under deducibility).

Perhaps someone will object that voluntary behaviour is much commoner than he thinks I am suggesting that it is. A person who acts out of beliefs and desires, the objector may say, can still act voluntarily, because his conduct is not the outcome of external forces or muscular reflexes, and may be not at all unwilling. Indeed even an infant or a dog may do something willingly rather than unwillingly, and on purpose rather than because of a reflex or accident.

There is a risk here of assuming that the everyday terminology of action is sharper and more determinate than it in fact is. Nevertheless the proposition that such-and-such a person is acting solely out of involuntary beliefs and desires does not imply that he is acting under external pressure, and I am not claiming that it does. The possibility that he acts voluntarily rather than involuntarily is certainly not ruled out by the involuntariness of his beliefs and desires. Nor is the possibility that he acts willingly rather than unwillingly. If he is indeed said to act voluntarily or willingly, the point is just that he does not mind, or quite likes, pursuing the purpose that he has come to have. He is not inclined to try and take steps that might dislodge the pertinent beliefs and desires or render them ineffective. If he were so inclined, that would make his action an unwilling one. But the action's unwillingness would not be identifiable with the involuntariness of his passive mental states. Of course in practice, except where they act out of habit or impulse, adult humans normally pay some evaluative consideration to the issues on which their beliefs and desires are focused. They thus transform the situation into one in which acceptance and goal-adoption play a part. And it is in this respect that they differ from infants and animals. No doubt a dog will often walk willingly rather than unwillingly, but that does not make its state of mind then voluntary rather than involuntary. Equally a dog may raise a paw on purpose rather than through the operation of a reflex. But this purpose—perhaps to obtain attention—is an outcome of belief and desire, not of acceptance and goal-adoption.

In sum, philosophers who have not grasped the importance of distinguishing between belief and acceptance, and have therefore not noticed the existence of correspondingly different kinds of purposive explanation, are inclined to deny that animals have beliefs.[6] These philosophers are intuitively aware that there is a vast structural difference between the explanation of animals' behaviour and the explanation of many human actions. So, since they analyse the latter solely in terms of beliefs and desires and since they can hardly deny that even animals have desires, they have to suppose that animals don't have beliefs: otherwise no structural difference between the explanation of animals' behaviour and the explanation of many human actions could be specified. But in fact, since animals are legitimately attributed beliefs (once belief is adequately distinguished from acceptance), we would be treating human adults just like animals if we were to insist that the driving force of their motivation, in each purposive act, is limited to the existence of relevant beliefs and desires in a certain pattern of inter-relationship.

Some consequences of all this may be usefully pursued a little further. So far as animals and pre-linguistic infants can believe but not accept, they are *a fortiori* not to be credited with the perform-ance of any action that implies the agent's mental acceptance of some corresponding proposition. In particular, to say that A has punished B for stealing is to imply that in the context A has accepted B's responsibility for the theft. So, if no acceptance at all

---

[6] For example, D. Davidson, *Inquiries into Truth and Interpretation* (Oxford: Clarendon Press, 1984), p. 170.

is possible on the part of a dog, we should not—literally—describe the dog as having punished the cat for eating its food. It will not do here to argue that, since the dog *believed* that the cat had eaten its food, appropriate conditions for its punishing the cat were established. For belief is neither necessary nor sufficient to constitute a punisher's appropriate mental state. It is not necessary since *A* may well believe that *B* is not responsible even though he accepts that he is. The innocent are sometimes punished quite knowingly, as when a judge rightly believes the accused to have been proven innocent even though he accepts the proposition that the jury has come to the opposite conclusion as his premiss for sentencing the accused to imprisonment for theft. And belief in *B*'s guilt is also not a sufficient condition for *A*'s being justified in punishing *B*. If *A*'s infliction of punishment is to be justified, he must, at least in the immediate context, adopt an appropriate premiss as the basis for a deliberate decision to bring about that punishment. That is, even if *A* believes in *B*'s guilt, he must also accept it.

§10. THE PURPOSES OF ORGANIZATIONS AND ARTEFACTS

It is to be noted that the distinctions discussed here cast some light on the senses in which communities, clubs, committees, corporations, nations, political parties, or other human organizations may be ascribed the possession of mental attitudes or the authorship of mental acts.

When a human organization of any kind is said to believe or desire that *p* this is normally a figurative way of saying summarily that most (if not all) of its individual members or most (if not all) of its official representatives believe or desire that *p*. On that purely distributive interpretation we can conceive activation of the relevant belief or desire as a feeling, without having to shoulder a heavy burden of philosophical or religious theory. For, if instead an organization like a company, community, or nation is said literally to believe or desire that *p* while at the same time most of its individual members and most of its official representatives are said not to believe or desire this, the organization is being ascribed a collective, self-conscious mind, and mental feelings of its own, within some appropriately metaphysical ontology.

But the position with acceptance and goal-seeking is quite different. So far as these are actions about which deliberation may take place and decisions be made, the possibility of carrying them out can be ascribed equally literally, and with an equally commonsensical ontology, either to an organization as a whole or to its individual members or representatives. Thus, just as a company or state can make its own promises, so too it can be committed (by legally appropriate procedures) to going along with the consequences of p as a basis for its collective decisions or for the acts of its agents in their official capacities, even though none of its members or representatives are so committed in relation to their private conduct. For example, a company may decide to conclude a contract with x, or a state may decide to conclude a treaty with y, on the basis of an official acceptance of x's or y's creditworthiness, even though the officials involved take care not to put any of their own money at risk thereby. Similarly, as a concession to threats or by a compromise decision, an organization or its duly-appointed agent can officially form an intention, or adopt a goal or policy, which most of its governing body seek to oppose by their actions in a private capacity. The conduct of these individuals may be hypocritical, cowardly, or incoherent. But it is by no means impossible or inconceivable, nor need its description have any metaphysical implications. Or a state may be committed to the acceptance of certain theological doctrines, along with whatever collectively celebrated religious rituals follow therefrom, even if few of its citizens have any corresponding beliefs or let those doctrines have any consequences for their private lives. Or two charitable foundations may have quite different purposes even though they have the same trustees.

In more traditional terminology, though still without any metaphysical implications, we could sum all this up by saying that an organized human group may exercise an active will or judgement of its own, and behave rationally or irrationally, even though it has no possibility of undergoing passive experiences of its own. Correspondingly, when anybody speaks literally in explaining a corporation's action in terms of its purposes, or in describing it as deliberating towards its decisions, or in holding it morally or legally responsible for its actions or for those of its agents, he should be construed as having in mind only what it wills and accepts, not what it desires or believes. Thus far, and no further, the corporation may be said to have a reality of its own, insomuch as its decisions and judgements enter into the explanatory order and are subject to the norms of rational choice. Indeed those who are averse to metaphysical ontologies and yet seek to construct an account of what they might informally and pre-theoretically call 'collective belief' will often, not unnaturally, find themselves in practice tending to use the vocabulary of acceptance rather than of belief within their analytical models, as Gilbert has recently done.[7]

Perhaps someone will object that this is altogether too restrictive. We feel no sense of metaphor, he may argue, when an airline is said to have lied to the public about its security practices or a college is said to be genuinely proud of its record at basketball. So the airline is being attributed belief-feelings that it does not reveal just as the college is implied to have feelings of pride. But, when we set on one side the beliefs of individual officials, what the lying airline conceals are such things as the conclusions that its own internal enquiry accepted, just as, when we set on one side the feelings of individual students or alumni, the college's pride in its basketball record boils down to a policy of advertising this record in its brochures. In other words when we look closely enough, and get behind the metaphor or the accidents of vocabulary, we find that organizations are typically engaged in accepting premises or pursuing goals, not in experiencing beliefs or desires. No doubt that is for two main reasons. First, organizations share with human adults the ability to formulate what they accept or decide in language. Consequently, their collective speech-acts (minuting of decisions and the reasons for decisions, publication of press-releases, adoption of accounts, etc.) are regulated by well-understood procedures and conventions, and their corporate actions (adherence to treaties, issue of new stock, etc.) admit of rational justification or condemnation in familiar terms. Secondly, an organization is not exposed at all to the chemical or physiological stimulation of feelings. We can experience feelings of trust, incredulity, love, hate, loyalty, jealousy, admiration or anger towards organizations. But they cannot experience any such feelings towards us.

---

[7] M. Gilbert, 'Modelling Collective Belief', *Synthese*, 73 (1987), pp. 185–204. Contrast, however, I. Levi, *Decisions and Revisions: Philosophical Essays on Knowledge and Value* (Cambridge: Cambridge University Press, 1934), p. 260.

In this way, within our ordinary conceptual system for purposive explanation, human organizations are treated in a way that is a kind of complementary opposite to that in which infants and animals are treated. Human organizations are credited with the capacity to accept propositions or adopt goals, but are implied to lack any capacity for believing or desiring. Infants and animals are credited with the latter capacity but not the former. Only normal adult humans (and, I suppose, creatures sufficiently like them elsewhere in the universe) are credited with both capacities. Only they can both act deliberately and have feelings. It follows that, in the computational models that are designed by cognitive psychologists to describe or explain how the adult human mind works, belief needs to be modelled distinctively alongside acceptance and desires alongside goal-adoptions. All four states of mind seem to occur—in many sub-varieties—and presumably each has its own biological functions.

Someone may be tempted to object here that computational psychology can in the end admit only acceptance, not belief. Digital computer programs, he may point out, can model—when they are run—any voluntary mental activity that is carried out sequentially in obedience to rules, has unbounded productivity, and is ultimately not a matter of degree but of on-off alternatives. They are therefore well suited to modelling acceptance, which is sequential (p. 14), voluntarily guided by consciously accepted rules (§4), subjectively closed under deducibility (§5), and not a matter of degree (pp. 114–16). And digital computer programs are also well suited to modelling the adoption of goals, since this too is open to guidance by rules, is capable of deductive closure within subjectively restricted limits, and is not a matter of degree. Correspondingly, such programs are not well suited to modelling beliefs, which can overlap one another in time (p. 14), which propagate and are propagated causally (§4), which are not deductively closed even from a subjective point of view (§5), and are matters of degree (§19). So, the objector concludes, the concept of belief is a figment of folk psychology: beliefs, in the sense defined, are unknown to contemporary science. And perhaps he would want to say the same thing about the concept of desire.

But the availability of connectionist models[8] undermines this

---

[8] See M. Boden, *Computer Models of Mind* (Cambridge: Cambridge University

objection. Successive states of a standard type of connectionist model can embrace massive parallel processing. They are linked causally, not by obedience to rules. They do not have unbounded productivity. And they function as an analogue computer, allowing graceful degradation (i.e. continuous decline from a maximal position). We can thus recognize their potential suitability for modelling belief or desire, and at the same time their obvious unsuitability for modelling acceptance or the adoption of goals.

It is not surprising, therefore, that some computational psychologists argue for the existence of at least two modes of cognitive operation: 'one rapid, efficient, subconscious, the other slow, serial and conscious'.[9] But the validity of such arguments about a factual issue is not at issue here. I am concerned expressly only with the legitimacy of certain conceptual distinctions. Nevertheless, in a matter in which the mind is both investigator and investigated one might well expect some kind of at least partial concordance eventually to arise in at least some cultures between the structure of the concepts employed in everyday human discourse and the structure of the facts that constitute a domain of application for those concepts and call, in turn, for scientific explanation. And, when the conceptual resources of contemporary Western folk psychology are properly appreciated, we can see an instance of such a concordance in the parallelism between the belief/acceptance duality in regard to folk-psychological concepts of cognitive states

---

Press, 1988); P. Smolensky, 'On the Proper Treatment of Connectionism', *Behavioral and Brain Sciences*, 11 (1988), pp. 1–23; J. A. Fodor and Z. W. Pylyshyn, 'Connectionism and Cognitive Architecture: A Critical Analysis', *Cognition*, 28 (1988), pp. 3–71; S. J. Hanson and D. J. Burr, 'What Connectionist Models Learn: Learning and Representation in Connectionist Networks', *Behavioral and Brain Sciences*, 13 (1990), pp. 471–518.

[9] D. A. Norman, 'Reflections on Cognition and Parallel Distributed Processing', in E. Rumelhart and J. L. McClelland (eds.), *Parallel Distributed Processing: Explorations in the Microstructure of Cognition*, vol. 2: *Psychological and Biological Models* (Cambridge, Mass.: MIT Press, 1986), p. 542. Compare the older distinction between automatic and attentional mental processes, e.g. M. I. Posner and C. R. Snyder, 'Attention and Cognitive Control', in R. L. Solso (ed.), *Information Processing and Cognition* (Hillsdale, NJ: Erlbaum, 1975), pp. 55–85; and R. M. Shiffria and W. Schneider, 'Controlled and Automatic Human Information Processing: Perceptual Learning, Automatic Attending and a General Theory', *Psychological Review*, 84 (1977), pp. 127–90. Some of the literature on hemispheric differences is also relevant: see G. M. Cohen, *The Psychology of Cognition* (London: Academic Press, 1983), pp. 234–50.

and the connectionist/digital duality in regard to scientific models of cognitive processes. Indeed, the existence of this parallelism counts as an argument for supposing that we should require our connectionist and digital models to explain our folk-psychological findings, instead of thinking it appropriate to reject the latter if they do not fit the former.[10]

What are we to say, however, about artificial intelligence projects that are intended to operate as substitutes for the exercise of human skills and attitudes rather than as part of the scientific description or explanation of human behaviour? An expert-system program that is designed to replace conscious, rule-following human activity in some area of recurrent problem-solving or decision-making, like medical diagnosis or portfolio management, is a program that exploits an accepted data-base in accordance with a humanly imposed set of goals, procedures, and policies. Beliefs and desires (and, indeed, any other dispositions to experience mental feelings about particular matters) are beside the point. And in fact the structure of the situation here is closely analogous to that affecting companies, states, and other human organizations. An organization is normally created to replace loosely associated or fully autonomous individuals in the execution of specialized tasks that are too large, too complex, or too controversial for such individual persons to perform satisfactorily within the time available. Division of labour takes the place of one-man bands, while job-descriptions, explicit regulation, and managerial supervision take the place of amateurish self-instruction and indifference to co-operation. And when specialized mental skills are to be usefully simulated in knowledge-engineering the rationale of the project is normally very similar. The skills are too extensive or too complex for live people to execute as accurately, efficiently, and coherently within the time available.

In short, it is not the so-called 'low-level' biological features of human cognition—the features shared with infants and animals—that digital-computational artefacts are best suited to simulate. It is rather certain 'high-level', rational features, such as calculating, proving, planning, premissing, inferring, or evaluating, that most appropriately admit of this. If humans can carry out a certain task consciously and under voluntary control inside their own minds, as in the case of these 'high-level' activities, they can reasonably hope to be able to design external mechanisms to execute that task. Analysis and articulation of the component procedures is always in principle possible, however difficult in practice.

Should we say then that such mechanisms are indeed calculating, proving, etc., or that they are just behaving as if they are calculating, proving, etc.? Should we say that the programmed artefact, not the physician, is diagnosing the patient's condition, or that the physician is diagnosing the condition by feeding relevant data into the artefact and interpreting its output? These, surely, are verbal issues. So far as the facts are concerned we can try to discover, by verifying the relevant programs, exactly what those programs achieve. We thus aim to discover the precise extent of the simulation that they render possible for their users or designers. And when we have indeed discovered this it seems then to be a much less important issue whether we can use the same terms to cover both the simulating and the simulated activities without any lapse into metaphor, or instead have to use different terms in order to emphasize the extent of what remains unsimulated.

But there will in any case remain one important element of disanalogy between the type of intelligent activity attributable to a human organization and the type attributable to a suitably programmed digital computer. A human organization is in principle capable of actually accepting a proposition or adopting a goal, as most legal systems recognize. To say that a particular corporation, for example, has merely simulated such an act is to raise doubts about its commercial probity. But all we expect our programmed computers, unattached to robots, to do in this context is either to simulate acts of acceptance or goal-adoption or to function as instruments of individuals or organizations that are performing such acts. No doubt this difference is connected with the fact that a human organization is readily credited with the same full-blooded linguistic competence as its rulers, governors, directors, or representatives, so that it is thought capable of asserting the propositions that it accepts, whereas under close examination digital computers are thought of as being primarily syntactic engines, are not credited with the semantic competence of their designers or users, and are therefore held incapable of actually asserting any propositions about the real world.[11] If instead computers existed only as components of language-learning robots, we might think differently of them.

These points have some bearing on the controversy between supporters and opponents of what Dennett calls the doctrine of 'original intentionality'.[12] According to that doctrine, only human beings (and perhaps some creatures like them on other planets) have an intrinsic, original, and underived capacity for purposive activity. Artefacts, like robots or chess-playing machines, that are designed by humans to engage in purposive activity, are attributed only a derived intentionality. And while Dennett sees himself with several distinguished allies, like the Churchlands, as opposing the doctrine, he classes Fodor, Searle, and many others as its supporters.

But once we grasp the diversity of structure that human purposive activity can have—and that use of the term 'intentionality' tends to conceal—we are on the road to resolving this controversy. On the one hand it is only adult humans (and perhaps some creatures like them on other planets) who standardly pursue purposes in terms of all the various possible combinations of belief, desire, acceptance, and intention. So adult human purposive activity has a concrete richness and complexity that make it the primary source for abstracting models and terminology with which to describe the activity of infants, animals, organizations, computers, robots, etc. On the other hand, without any necessary recourse to metaphor, explanation in terms of acceptance and goal-seeking may legitimately be employed in abstraction from the beliefs and desires that normally interconnect with them in human activity. In suitable cases we can discern the relevance of such explanations to the behaviour of organizations and even to that of programmed artefacts.

§11. SOME CONNECTIONS BETWEEN EXPLANATION AND DELIBERATION

The analytical points that I have been making do not bear solely on explanations—that is, on the retrospective understanding of a person's actions. They bear also on prospective reasonings.

[11] L. J. Cohen, *The Dialogue of Reason* (Oxford: Clarendon Press, 1986), pp. 208–9.
[12] *The Intentional Stance*, pp. 289–95.

First, they bear on predictions about the behaviour of others. Knowing a person's relevant beliefs and desires we may be able to predict what he will do next. Knowing what his beliefs are and what he is going to do we may be able to predict his desires. Knowing what his desires are and what he is going to do we may be able to predict his beliefs. But if we take into account what a person accepts, and the goals at which he is aiming, several additional patterns of predictive reasoning become possible— parallel to the patterns of explanatory reasoning already discussed. Philosophers who ignore this point are forced either, like Dennett, to endorse applications of just the same 'intentional stance' to persons and to animals,[13] or alternatively, like Davidson, to argue that animals do not even have beliefs.[14]

Secondly, these considerations are crucial to a person's delibera- tive reasoning about his own future actions. If explanations in terms of beliefs and desires are to be construed as citing involuntary mental states, we must reject the view that deliberation towards a decision can be conducted wholly in *those* terms. For a person in a quandary to have regard solely to his own beliefs and desires, as such, would be for him to behave as if he were predicting what someone else will do rather than deciding what he himself will do. He would be looking on himself as an object rather than a subject, as a passive experiencer rather than an active agent. To think of oneself as still making up one's mind whether or not to do act *A*, one must have regard instead primarily to the acceptability of certain relevant propositions, or to the value of achieving relevant goals, or to the combination of these issues. The question to be asked of oneself is 'Should I accept that *p*?', not 'Do I believe that *p*?', or 'Should I adopt *x* as my goal?', not 'Do I desire *x*?' So, despite Ramsey's own formulation of the matter (see §19 below), the conception of probability that is most germane to decision theory, as a technology of adult human action, is one that measures accepted risk that *p* rather than one that measures strength of belief that *p*. And the most germane conception of utility is one that measures the priority or importance assigned to the achievement of relevant goals rather than one that measures associated feelings of mental or bodily pleasure. Correspondingly the conceptions of

---

[13] Ibid. pp. 13–35.
[14] *Inquiries into Truth and Interpretation*, p. 170.

probability and utility that are most germane to the description or explanation of rationally deliberated decisions (for example, on economic issues) are those that measure the accepted risk that the relevant propositions are true and the value assigned to adopting the relevant goals, respectively. On the other hand, we may conceive the purposive activity of infants or animals to be swayed by the balance of their dispositions, so that explanations of the activity in terms of belief and desire can exploit differences of degree in those states of mind, as oriented towards different states of affairs. We might need then to apply in such explanations some measure of the strength of belief that p rather than of the accepted risk that p and a conception of utility that measures feelings of pleasure or desire-satisfaction rather than assignments of priority.

Thirdly, it is worth considering how we persuade someone else to act in a particular way. At the simplest, we need to draw his attention to those facts that will provide an appropriate basis for his deliberations. If, for example, his overriding goal is to buy the cheapest car that is on the market, he will come to buy a model Z if he accepts our claim that model Z is in fact the cheapest. But in this respect our intervention will not have *caused* him to buy a model Z, any more than his own deliberations caused him to do so—at least in that sense of 'cause' in which every individual event of causation instantiates some causal law. Acceptance is a voluntary act and when he accepts, in his deliberations, that model Z is cheapest—either because he has discovered the fact for himself or because we have told him it—he is not thereby giving way to some overwhelming causal force that is being exercised on him by belief in the cheapness of model Z. Nor, when he decides to buy a model Z, is he giving way to some overwhelming causal force that is exercised on him by this acceptance. By accepting that model Z is cheapest he has already in fact committed himself to that decision, in virtue of his having adopted the goal of buying the cheapest car that is on the market. Indeed, the connection between his acceptance and his decision is a logical rather than a causal one, just because—within his grasp of such connections—acceptance and goal-adoption are both deductively closed. And it is in keeping with the absence of any implied causal connection here that our car-buyer could even turn out to change his mind and go back on his commitment before he finally signs the cheque. He certainly might come to reject the claim that model Z is cheapest, or he might come to reject the goal of buying the cheapest car. More importantly, he could also do neither of those things and yet still not buy the car. Then no doubt he is being irrational. But he is still not breaking, or constituting an exception to, any supposed causal law.

It would be quite different if you were said to be playing on someone's passively experienceable beliefs and desires, irrespective of what he accepts or of the goals that he adopts. Perhaps you try to use subliminal advertising in order to persuade him that model Z is the best buy. Or perhaps you tell him that his favourite film-star drives one, since you know that he associates every virtue with her. One way or another you (metaphorically) pull the right levers, and press the right buttons, and thus you cause him to buy a model Z. Of course, in practice, even after a great deal of high-pressure salesmanship, he might still fail to buy the car. But then his failure to do so could be said to falsify the causal generalization that you had been taught on your salesmanship course. What you thought was a causal law is not one after all, and you need to improve your technique in order to be more successful next time. Not that it is at all easy to find intuitively plausible examples of such causal processes in adult human life (as distinct from that of infants or animals). That is because in practice, as already remarked, people not acting out of habit normally pay some evaluative consideration to their beliefs and desires and thus transform the situation into one in which acceptance and goal-adoption are operative factors.

§12. REASONS AND CAUSES

An important consequence of all this is that the much-discussed philosophical question 'Are reasons causes?' is radically ambiguous and does not admit of a single answer. In one main sense of this word 'reason'—perhaps a rather Pickwickian one—we can treat the question as a problem about explanation in terms of beliefs and desire-type attitudes: is such explanation causal? And it is clear that in that sense the question requires an affirmative answer. Purposive explanation is causal there, since the relations involved in the genesis of the action to be explained are causal—as we saw in the case of infants or animals, or of adults induced to buy cars by high-pressure salesmanship. But, where the explanation is in terms of acceptance and goal-adoption, or of similarly voluntary mental states, it is equally clear that the reasons given retrospectively for a particular action, when the explainer says what was accepted and what was aimed at, are no more causal factors than are the reasons that a person may have in mind prospectively in the course of his deliberations that culminated in a decision to do the action. Indeed, when afterwards the agent himself tells us his reasons for so acting, setting out a practical syllogism in terms of the facts (minor premiss) that he accepted and the goals (major premiss) that he pursued, he is certainly giving us a non-causal explanation of the action. By showing us that the action was the rational one—or at least a reasonable one—to do in his case he justifies it pragmatically and thus explains it (though he may not be justifying it in moral terms, since his goal may have been thoroughly reprehensible). He explains it because his justification will enable any other agent, with an analogous capacity for rational action, to understand why he did what he did. And, if this rationality-based explanation is not given by him but by someone else, it will be just as correct and should be just as productive of understanding.

Accordingly, philosophers like Davidson who claim that understanding the reasons for an action is essentially understanding its causation[15] are being no less mistakenly one-sided than are philosophers like Melden who claim that the explanation for an action is always related to it by some kind of logical connection.[16] In order to dispel the unnecessary controversy here what is needed is to avoid confusing belief with acceptance or desire with goal-adoption and thus to recognize that at least two focal patterns of purposive explanation are available. For dealing with animals or infants the appropriate pattern is causal and relates actions to beliefs and desires. For dealing with human organizations the appropriate pattern is logical and rational, relating actions to accepted premisses and to adopted goals or policies. And for dealing with adult humans both patterns are available (along with their hybrids). On any particular occasion of adult human action the more appropriate pattern of purposive explanation is determined by the extent to which the agent has let himself be dominated by his situation or has instead managed to dominate it himself.

Indeed, on many—perhaps most—occasions of adult human action both types of explanation will be applicable, even if to differing degrees, because on those occasions what the agent believes is coextensive with what he accepts and what he desires is coextensive with the goal that he adopts. And if, in the explanation of a particular act, what is said to be the agent's causally operative belief is different from what is said to be his accepted reason for the act, or what is said to be the agent's driving desire is different from what he is said to have adopted as a goal, then the citation of reasons in terms of acceptance and goal-adoption will appear as a rationalization rather than as a genuine explanation. This generally happens, for example, when the agent's relevant belief or desire is held to be an unconscious or subconscious one—i.e. to be a (perhaps Freudian) disposition that is not manifested in introspective consciousness but is only inferable from what the agent says or does.

Of course there are in practice many degrees and varieties of these and similar explanations. Perhaps one type of explanation that deserves special mention in this context is the explanation of certain actions in terms of rules or roles to which the agents view themselves as voluntarily conforming. Here conformity to such-or-such a rule may be regarded as a goal of the agent, and the explanatory pattern is thus to be seen, in that context, as a justificational rather than a causal one. The agent obeys the relevant rule when he accepts that the situation is of the kind to which it applies. So his action could be justified by his adoption of the rule and his acceptance of the situation. The importance of this way of explaining an action is rightly emphasized by certain philosophers.[17] But it is equally important to recognize that commitment to its use wherever appropriate does not exclude other types of explanation from being appropriate elsewhere.

It should also be emphasized that in appropriate contexts the two hybrid types of explanation mentioned earlier (pp. 48–9) are available. Specifically it may sometimes be necessary to relate what is accepted to what is desired, on the one hand, or what is believed

---

[17] For example, P. Winch, *The Idea of a Social Science and its Relation to Philosophy* (London: Routledge and Kegan Paul, 1958).

to what is intended, on the other. Thus a person's working harder may be due to his acceptance of the premiss that working harder will bring about the satisfaction of his desire for promotion, or to his belief that working harder will accomplish his plan to achieve promotion. Curiously Bratman[18] has taken the second of these two hybrid patterns of explanation to be the one that most characteristically applies to the behaviour of rational agents, and has ignored altogether the pattern that cites acceptance and intention. He rightly contrasts explanatory references to plans or intentions with explanatory references to desires, and he rightly stresses the greater relevance of the former for the analysis of practical reasoning. But he fails to notice the role of the concept of acceptance in our explanations of human behaviour, and so he wrongly takes the relation of belief to intention as being central to practical reasoning.

Finally it has also to be emphasized that the richness of our conceptual resources for explaining one another's actions, as for interpreting one another's thoughts, should not lead us to conjure up a dualistic metaphysical foundation for those resources. We should not say, for example, that there is a causal, deterministic order within which such dispositions as belief, doubt, desire, and repugnance hold sway, and a realm of reason and free-will in which propositions are accepted or rejected and goals are adopted or repudiated. We should not say this because all the mental states concerned are intricately intertwined with one another, as we have seen, in the single world of everyday reality. Indeed, the prevalence of just such metaphysical dualisms—from the seventeenth to the early twentieth century—may sometimes have been what provoked empirically-minded philosophers to propose against them an apparently hard-headed, though actually over-simplified, monistic analysis that confined the concept of purpose to states combining appropriately interconnected beliefs and desires. In reacting against that analytical over-simplification we must avoid any temptation to relapse into the kind of speculative ontological extravagance that may have originally provoked it. What is necessary is just to stress the importance of the difference between the one type of mental state and the other, and the need to represent this difference adequately in any relevant descriptions, simulations, or explana-

[18] M. E. Bratman, *Intention, Plans and Practical Reason* (Cambridge, Mass.: Harvard University Press, 1987), p. 31.

tions that we construct. Terms in the one vocabulary pick out those features of mental life that, being passive, admit of profitable investigation into their causes and effects. Terms in the other vocabulary pick out those features that, since they commence with decisions or the formation of intentions, can be regarded as actions for a reason. Features of the former type correlate readily with one another in patterns of causal uniformity that hold good under normal conditions. Features of the latter type are logically relevant to one another in patterns of deliberative reasonableness.

There is, of course, a further problem about the relation between either type of mental state, on the one hand, and underlying neurological processes on the other. But that problem does not need to be tackled in the present context.

III
What Cognitive State Does Indicative Speech Express?

This chapter takes up the question: when someone says that p, what is the cognitive state that he commits himself to having—belief or acceptance? The issue is first (§13) discussed in relation to Moore's Paradox and the difference between statements and assertions. The next section (§14) enquires whether there are other, co-ordinate cognitive states to which saying that p may commit its author, and connects the enquiry with problems about discovering the semantics of exotic languages. The final section (§15) investigates Stich's claim that the current list of cognitive states that can actually underlie our utterances does not even include belief.

§13. THE DIFFERENCE BETWEEN STATEMENTS AND ASSERTIONS

It is widely held that, in normal everyday-life situations, when someone says 'It is raining' with an affirmative intonation, he implies (in the sense of 'gives it to be understood') that he believes that it is raining—and analogously for other indicative sentences. Indeed, that thesis, or something very like it, is commonly offered as being crucial to the understanding of what is called 'Moore's Paradox'.[1] The thesis is said to explain why it seems odd or anomalous for someone to say:

It is raining, but I do not believe that it is raining.

Clearly the two clauses of such an utterance are not logical contradictories of one another, since both could well be true. So the intuitive oddity cannot be due to the utterance's being logically self-contradictory. But the intuitive oddity of the utterance can apparently be explained by supposing that—normally—by utter-

---

[1] G. E. Moore, *Ethics* (London: Williams and Norgate, 1912), p. 125.

ing the first clause the speaker implies that he believes that it is raining, whereas by uttering the second clause he explicitly denies that he believes this (just as by uttering the first clause the speaker explicitly affirms that it is raining, whereas by uttering the second clause he implicitly denies that it is). The implication of the speaker's saying what he does, in one part of his utterance, is thus supposed to clash with what he says explicitly in another part of the same utterance.

That understanding of Moore's Paradox needs to be modified, however, if it is wrong to hold that a person's saying that it is raining standardly implies that he believes that it is raining. And I shall now argue that this kind of implication (or conversational implicature,[2] if you prefer that terminology) exists only in some types of everyday situation and not in others.

We have to bear in mind here the differences between belief and acceptance that have already been described. So let us examine whether saying that it is raining standardly implies belief that it is raining, or whether it may not instead quite often imply acceptance that it is raining.

Some familiar types of speech-act clearly tend to imply belief. That is, the description of an utterance in certain terms normally entails that the utterance implies the corresponding belief. For example, suppose the utterance is correctly described as a 'statement'. Of course, I don't mean that it's describable as a statement only in the sense of that word in which about fifty or sixty years ago the word became a technical term for many philosophers, defined sometimes as signifying a truth-value bearing sentence-in-use[3] and apparently welcomed as a less metaphysical-sounding substitute for the term 'proposition'. To describe an utterance as the utterance of a statement in that sense tells us little about what is or ought to be the speaker's mental attitude towards this proposition, alias 'statement', just as it tells us little about the force of the utterance or about the speech-act that the utterance is intended to execute. But consider instead the still current non-technical sense of the word 'statement' in which it entails the

---

[2] See H. P. Grice, 'Logic and Conversation', in D. Davidson and G. Harman (eds.), *The Logic of Grammar* (Encino, Calif.: Dickinson, 1975), pp. 64–75.

[3] For example, P. F. Strawson, *Introduction to Logical Theory* (London: Methuen, 1952); J. L. Austin, *How to Do Things with Words* (Oxford: Clarendon Press, 1962), pp. 1–4.

authoritative informativeness of an utterance, its conformity with appropriate standards of formality, or the implicit willingness of the speaker to stand behind it. In this sense it functions as a term of pragmatics, not semantics. For example, persons who are suspected of crimes or have witnessed accidents are asked to provide the police with statements, politicians are said to issue statements at press conferences or to make them to their legislatures, banks offer to send out regular statements to customers about their accounts, applicants for passports are asked to state their names, ages, addresses and occupations, and so on. So an utterance correctly describable as a statement in this sense is one that would normally imply—i.e. give it to be understood—that a corresponding belief or web of beliefs exists in the mind of the speaker. If you make an alibi statement to the police, for example, you imply that you believe what you say and that this belief is sufficiently coherent with your other beliefs for you to be reasonably confident of its truth. You have not just decided, perhaps for reasons of your own convenience, to take the proposition that *p* as a premiss. Rather, you imply that you are declaring what you honestly and spontaneously feel to be true independently of your own decisions. The police may believe you if they take you yourself to believe what you say, or they might even think that you had made a mistake. But in normal circumstances they will certainly not believe you if they don't take you yourself to believe what you say. So, since a normal part of the point of making a statement is to get your hearers to believe you, the speech-act of making a statement normally implies that the speaker possesses the corresponding belief or web of beliefs. The more emphatic the statement, the stronger—or the more important—the belief that is implied. The issuance of a printed bank-statement implies that the officials who issue it believe firmly in its accuracy. And something similar can be said about reports, warnings, narrations, declarations, and testimonies. If you testify falsely that *p*, for example, you are open to the charge of dishonesty, or even of perjury, if you do not yourself believe that *p*. Perhaps you have sworn to tell nothing but the truth when you testify that *p*, while, if you do not believe that *p*, you are certainly telling something that you yourself do not feel to be true.

But obviously none of this can apply to speech-acts expressing acceptance. When a person says, for example, 'I hereby accept that *p*, i.e., I take that proposition as a premiss for any relevant decision or argument', he does not imply that he also believes—i.e. is disposed to feel—that *p*, and the same must therefore be true when his just saying that *p* is correctly described as a speech-act of acceptance. Analogously assertions, concessions, agreements, acknowledgements, and admissions are all speech-acts that may be performed, in appropriate contexts, by the utterance of an affirmatively intoned indicative sentence without implying the existence of the corresponding belief.

Of course, I am not using 'assertion' here in any technical sense that may, or may not, be relevant to understanding the function of Frege's so-called 'assertion-sign'. Rather, I am concerned with assertions in the ordinary, non-technical sense of the word, in which they involve the declaration of a claim and some expectation of its recognition or insistence on its validity. For example, you might assert your ownership of a piece of land, your lack of skill at chess, or your fondness for cheese. In this sense of 'assertion' the conditions warranting an assertion that *p* are not necessarily the same as, though they often overlap with, those warranting a statement that *p*. For example, you may be criticized for asserting instead of arguing that *p*, rather than for stating instead of arguing that *p*. But the police would not normally ask you to make an assertion about an accident, nor would you ask your bank for an assertion of your account, though in both cases it would be quite in order to request a statement and the requester might regard part of what was given him as a mistaken assertion. A statement may come to be considered an assertion only in a context in which the question of a possible challenge to the statement has somehow been raised. Again, being assertive on an issue depends on the nature of what you say about it, rather than on a proneness to making a lot of statements about it. Even if numerous, your statements might all be so carefully hedged that they seem to be rather unassertive. So in this sense there is no reason at all why an assertion that *p* should normally imply that the speaker believes that *p*. He may well be insisting on recognition of his claim that *p* because he wants people to know that he accepts that *p*, though he lacks as yet—and perhaps will never have—any corresponding belief. He may even have no evidence that *p*, and his acceptance and assertion that *p* may be just out of loyalty to an old friend who has testified that *p*. It is thus very far from being the case that, as

Dummett claims, 'assertion is rightly called an expression of belief'.[4]

Perhaps this absence of any implication about belief may be easier for you to recognize in the case of concessions, agreements, acknowledgements, and admissions than in the case of assertions, because so many philosophers have for so long just taken it for granted that assertions that *p* imply beliefs that *p*. For certainly, if in the course of a dispute or debate I concede that *p*, I am agreeing that the proposition that *p* may be used as a premiss for further argument about the fact in dispute. But that fact may well be quite independent of my own state of belief. We may be arguing about other issues than about what I believe. It might therefore be quite irrelevant to imply anything about my beliefs, and the conventional point of the utterance might be secured without exploiting any such implication. Nor would it be in any way dishonest or insincere if in the course of settling a dispute I conceded that *p* while still self-confessedly believing that not-*p*. The conditions warranting the occurrence of concessions are thus certainly very different from those warranting the occurrence of statements, reports, narrations, or testimonies.

Moreover, when the nature of such a speech-act is clear from its context it does not have to be made linguistically evident by the performative use of expressions like 'I concede that . . . ', 'I agree that . . . ', etc. (though the possibility of the latter form of expression reinforces the relevant intuitions). So it is hardly deniable that, in quite a wide range of familiar indicative-mood speech-acts, saying that *p* does not imply belief that *p*. Rather it implies there a mental act of acceptance that *p*. Concessions, agreements, acknowledgements, admissions, and assertions are all concerned in one way or another with the adoption of premises rather than with the expression of feelings.

What then should we say about Moore's Paradox? If what has been said is correct, sentences like

It is raining but I do not believe that it is raining

cannot be quite as odd or anomalous as most philosophers who have discussed them have supposed. Where the utterance of 'It is raining' implies acceptance that it is raining but not belief that it is raining, there should be no feeling of oddness or anomaly. And in

---

[4] M. Dummett, *Frege's Philosophy of Language* (London: Duckworth, 1973), p. 330. Compare also B. Williams, *Problems of the Self* (Cambridge: Cambridge University Press, 1973), p. 137.

fact it is not at all difficult to imagine such cases with more complex structures, as in

All right. Your arguments from economic theory are unanswerable and I have to concede your point. Index-linked wage settlements are inflationary. But, although I am bound to accept this, and everything that follows from it, I still don't really *believe* that index-linked wage settlements are inflationary.

As so often in linguistic analysis, a larger slab of discourse constrains us to suppose a speech-act that is different from the one that a smaller slab suggests. Correspondingly, if we want to ensure that the type of oddity or anomaly at issue is involved in the utterance of the sentence we cite, we have apparently to consider some such sentence as

It is raining but I neither believe nor accept that it is raining.

§14. DO THE CONCEPTS OF BELIEF AND ACCEPTANCE EXHAUST THEIR GENUS?

This kind of amplification naturally raises the question whether there is any other category of cognitive attitude, on a par with belief and acceptance and not just a species of one or the other, which may be implied by the utterance of indicative sentences with an affirmative intonation. Or is it sufficient to say merely, 'I neither believe nor accept that it is raining', alongside 'It is raining', in order to produce the anomaly?

Perhaps, for example, taking it as a conclusion that p should be thought in this context to be comparable with taking it as a premiss that p, and then there will be a case for treating inference that p as being co-ordinate with acceptance or belief that p. But can you definitively infer that p without also accepting that p? In other words, can you honestly treat the proposition that p as an established conclusion if you are not ready to take it as a premiss for further argumentation in appropriate circumstances? If not, acceptance has a certain priority, since one can certainly accept that p without having inferred that p.

Or perhaps involuntarily taking it as a premiss that p should be thought contrastable with voluntarily taking it as a premiss that p, i.e. with acceptance. If so, there is apparently a third category of mental attitude that is on a par with belief and acceptance, as analysed here, and may therefore be implied by the utterance of indicative sentences. But how could it be possible for someone's taking it as a premiss that p to be an involuntary act? Other people may force you to make bodily movements that they want you to make, but they cannot force you to construct the inferences that they want. Forcing you to write down a syllogism is not at all the same as forcing you to make the corresponding inference in your own mind. And, though your feelings about taking the proposition that p as a premiss are undoubtedly involuntary, just as is your feeling that it is true that p, the issue about whether you actually do take the proposition that p as a premiss is not necessarily determined by those feelings. When you think that there are objective, evidential reasons in favour of accepting that p, you may decide to take the proposition that p as a premiss even though it saddens, angers, or even disgusts you to do so. Accordingly, we cannot hold involuntarily taking it as a premiss that p to be a third category of mental attitude that is on a par with belief and acceptance.

There is also a powerful reason to suppose that, in at least one important respect, belief and acceptance constitute a duopoly of human thought. I have in mind here the range of states of mind that need to be imputed to the speaker of an exotic language when we try to discover its semantics from his behaviour. Of course, his apparent fears, hopes, wishes, joys, disappointments, embarrassments, and other emotional or affective states are also relevant. Without making plausible assumptions about when these are occurring we cannot expect to form plausible hypotheses about the states of affairs that the native speaker believes or premisses to exist and correspondingly has occasion to represent in his linguistic utterances. If he is suddenly afraid, his utterance is more likely to be warning us of the tiger whose tracks he has just detected than to be sympathizing with us about the heat. Apparent motive helps to indicate the nature and content of the speech-act. But the act of saying that such-or-such is the case is the key linguistic feature of so many utterances that the states of mind underlying those acts may reasonably be regarded as constituting an outstandingly important category. At any rate, if there is a methodology for investigating an exotic language (or even for explaining human action) that can dispense with the explicit or implicit inclusion of this category within its taxonomy, the methodology has yet to be made public. To put the point in terms of Indo-European grammar, there is a vital role for the cognitive states that are normally and characteristically expressed by the utterance of indicative sentences.

So, if we want to establish the range of co-ordinate variation that exists within this category of states of mind, we might usefully look at the variety of evidence that we need in order to be able to construct a semantics for indicative sentences. Since exotic languages have in fact often been given decodings that are universally agreed to be reasonably satisfactory, there must often, *pace* Quine,[5] be sufficient evidence somehow for this agreement to be justified.

Now a semantics for the indicative sentences of a natural language has two main elements, even though over the past forty years or so these two elements have not always been given equal emphasis. Part of the semantics must be concerned with the relation of those sentences to the facts of the non-linguistic world and part with their relations to one another. Thus one part would ideally deploy, for each sentence, the various conditions under which its utterance would express a true proposition and another part would deploy the various relations of entailment and contradiction that lie between the propositions expressed by different sentences. Philosophers have indeed often pointed out that knowledge which does not extend beyond inter-sentential relationships, so as to articulate a system of truth-conditions, is insufficient to enable anyone to use a language appropriately on particular occasions or to understand how it is being so used. They have perhaps not quite as often drawn attention to the complementary truism, namely that knowledge which does not extend beyond truth-conditions, so as to articulate a system of entailments and contradictions, is insufficient to enable anyone to converse coherently or to understand the full implications of what is said. One needs to know not only the conditions under which it is true to say that George is Peter's brother but the implication therefrom that George and Peter have the same parents, that anyone else who is a brother of George is also a brother of Peter, and so on. In short, semantical knowledge

---

[5] W. V. O. Quine, *Word and Object* (Cambridge, Mass.: MIT Press, 1960), pp. 26–79.

—in regard to non-modal indicative sentences—has an inherent duality of structure.

It is of no importance for present purposes to theorize about how such semantical knowledge can best be formulated. There are problems, for instance, about how a Davidsonian semantics can cope plausibly with the inherent polysemy of natural-language predicates,[6] and problems too about how to articulate the systemic structure of natural-language entailments.[7] The point to be made here is just that, however difficult it may be to write a comprehensive semantics for a natural language's indicative sentences, there is no doubt that their truth-conditions and their entailments constitute the two main types of feature that such a semantics would need to reveal.

But now the connection with belief and acceptance should be evident. If we hypothesize about the native speaker's belief, we hypothesize about what—in the given situation—he feels to be true, and we may go on to hypothesize on that basis about the truth-conditions for the indicative sentence that he utters as his statement, report, warning, etc. in the situation. These are the conditions that, when he has the relevant belief, he feels to be satisfied. Similarly, if we hypothesize about what the native speaker accepts in a particular situation, we hypothesize about what he premisses therefrom and we may go on to hypothesize accordingly about what is entailed or contradicted by the indicative sentences that he utters. And in both cases our hypotheses are subject to indefinitely many possible revisions or corrections in the light of further relevant information. We may discover, for example, that our informant was not drawing attention to the whole tiger but only to its claws, which he *believed* to fit the tracks. Or we may discover that he was drawing our attention to Peter's relationship by marriage, so that what he was *accepting*, as later remarks make clear, was that George is Peter's brother-in-law. Accordingly the point that emerges is that this structural duality in our semantical knowledge echoes the underlying duopoly of cognitive attitude. And we should no more expect to find other cognitive attitudes that are co-ordinate with belief and acceptance in respect of being

---

[6] L. J. Cohen, 'A Problem about Ambiguity in Truth-Theoretical Semantics', *Analysis*, 45 (1985), pp. 129–34.

[7] L. J. Cohen, 'Chess as a Model of Language', *Philosophia*, 11 (1982), pp. 51–87.

implied by the utterance of indicative sentences, than we should expect to find other dimensions of indicative-sentence meaning that are co-ordinate with truth-conditions and entailments. Or, at least, if you want to claim that there is another such cognitive attitude, you need to be able to characterize the dimension of indicative-sentence meaning for the study of which we normally identify and investigate instances of this other state of mind.

The point can be made about normative or evaluative thinking, as well as about opinion on matters of fact. We can distinguish two polar modes of moral evaluation, for example, about how things ought to be. On the one hand people may be disposed to experience dictates of conscience or feelings of moral indignation, and these involuntary dispositions can be regarded as forms of belief, whether about general issues or about particular ones. On the other hand, they may voluntarily come to adopt principles or ideals which then function, in effect, as premises for their practical reasoning in particular situations; or they may just come to accept a reasoned judgement about a particular issue. But the same natural language sentence, with the very same meaning (for example, 'It is wrong for the rich not to give to the poor'), may express either state of mind. So here too we should expect that the semantics of the natural-language sentence will be adequately understood only when the underlying mental duality is properly grasped.

Note, however, that this expectation does not commit us to a naturalistic or descriptivist analysis of moral terms. Statements of the truth-conditions for moral evaluations have to relate those evaluations to what is actually right or wrong, irrespective of how the concepts of rightness and wrongness should be analysed. 'It is wrong for the rich not to give to the poor' is true if and only if it is wrong for the rich not to give to the poor. Indeed the variety of analyses that have been offered for moral terms no doubt rests in part on the difference between the two main kinds of mental state that underlie their use. Emotive or intuitionist theories reflect the involuntary role of moral belief, while utilitarian or Kantian theories stress rather the importance of adopting the right premises in moral reasoning.

Some philosophers may be inclined to object here that I am wrongly assuming mental states to be prior, in relevant respects, to the corresponding speech-acts. Thus instead of viewing assertion as the expression of a certain interior act of judgement, it will be said, one ought rather to view judgement as the 'interiorization' of that external convention-bound act of assertion. And the reason for this may be alleged to be that an act constituted by a social convention can be described without circularity as the expression of a mental state or mental act only if there exist non-conventional ways of expressing that mental state or act. If such non-conventional forms of expression do not exist, no prior mental state or act is identifiable. Greeting, for example, has such forms of expression, but judgement—for the most part—has not. As Dummett writes, 'We can describe the convention governing a gesture of greeting by saying that it is used as an expression of pleasure at seeing somebody, only because it is possible to express such pleasure without the use of the conventional gesture. Most judgements, however, it would be senseless to ascribe to someone who had not a language capable of expressing them, because there is no "natural" behaviour which, taken by itself, is enough to express those judgements.'[8]

Here again, however, the difference between belief and acceptance is crucial.

People express their beliefs in very many non-conventional ways. By carrying an umbrella, for example, you are normally taken to express your belief that it may well rain that day. But the disposition to act in appropriate ways that normally accompanies and expresses the belief that p is not to be equated with this belief (pp. 8–11). So there is room for certain kinds of statement and of similar forms of speech-act to be non-circularly described as expressing beliefs. And in such cases the belief—identified by its association with a disposition to act accordingly—might indeed be said to be prior to any speech-act that also expresses the belief (just as the belief—identified by its association with a disposition to speak accordingly—might also be said to be prior to any actions that express the belief). Nor is it at all paradoxical that belief-feelings should be expressable in ways that are not constituted by social convention. In this respect they are just like other kinds of feeling. By clambering down the river-bank, for example, a thirsty animal shows its desire to drink and its belief in the presence of water.

But acceptance is another matter. To take it as a premiss that p one needs to be able somehow to spell out or articulate the proposition that p, as is done in oral communication, in sub-vocal

---

[8] Dummett, *Frege's Philosophy of Language*, p. 362.

speech, or in some other convention-bound way. How else can one's conclusions be supposed to be tied to the component elements of one's premisses? How else can they be exhibited as a transformation of—or derivation from—those premisses according to logical, conceptual, or mathematical rules?

It is reasonable therefore to view any kind of acceptance as an interiorization of the corresponding speech-act. Indeed we saw earlier (in §9) that, in order to explain their behaviour in familiar terms, infants and animals may be attributed appropriate beliefs and desires despite having no language, but that they cannot plausibly be said to accept that so-and-so or to adopt such-or-such a goal or policy. And what is being said now fits in with this, because it views the rudiments of belief, but not of acceptance, as capable of existing prior to language. Correspondingly, *pace* Dummett, it is defensible to describe judgement as an interiorization only so far as 'judgement' means acceptance rather than belief.

Nevertheless, even after all this has been said, it is not true in every context that belief has to be treated as being less language-bound than acceptance is. In particular, for heuristic purposes, in a context in which you are investigating the semantics of an exotic language, your hypotheses about a native speaker's beliefs and your hypotheses about his acceptances will be equally fundamental to your investigations, since knowledge of indicative sentences' truth-conditions and knowledge of their implications are equally indispensable components of a speaker-hearer's semantical competence.

§15. DOES BELIEF EXIST?

So far, in exploring the everyday, folk-psychological concepts of belief and acceptance I have assumed that both concepts are non-empty. I have assumed, for example, that purposive explanations are sometimes true and therefore that the beliefs or acceptances which they postulate do actually occur in people's minds. And I have assumed that sincere and honest statements and assertions are sometimes made and therefore that the beliefs or acceptances which they express are real. But according to Stich[9] there are

---

[9] S. P. Stich, *From Folk Psychology to Cognitive Science: The Case against Belief* (Cambridge, Mass.: MIT Press, 1983).

promising arguments against the view that belief is ever a state or property of a person's mind. How good are those arguments?

Most of them are concerned with much-discussed general problems about the role of indirect discourse as an instrument in the articulation or characterization of mental content. And such problems affect memory, hope, fear, desire, grief, joy, acceptance, and a wide range of other concepts just as much as they affect belief. So the resolution of those problems is neither eased nor made harder (see §6) by the distinction between belief and acceptance. Their resolution therefore falls outside the scope of the present book. It is merely assumed to be possible. For we should be rejecting too much—within the field of psychology—of what we normally take as data that require explanation, if our arguments lead us to suppose that the idioms of indirect discourse have no role whatever to perform in the characterization of mental reality. It may well be the case that those idioms have no role to perform in the construction of explanatory theories that satisfy the criteria of merit by conformity to which the natural sciences have made such striking progress. It might also be the case that different cultures divide up the mental spectrum differently, with some exotic conceptual systems recognizing mental states or attitudes that we do not recognize, or not recognizing some that we do.[10] Perhaps some languages even lack any idioms for indirect discourse. But it would remain an *ignoratio elenchi* to suppose that no mental states have articulatable content, since the make-up of human memories, hopes, fears, desires, etc. constitutes such a familiar part of what needs to be explained by any scientific psychology. If, for example, Freud gave us an unsatisfactory explanation of why we forget much of our infant experience or of why some people have certain types of false belief about their parents, we need a better explanation. And, if other cultures present some unfamiliar data, that is a reason for saying that psychological theory has more to explain than was previously thought to be the case, not for saying that not even familiar data are to be taken seriously.

Stich has another argument which is based on what he calls 'the sorry history of folk theories in general'.[11] But the fact that Newton

---

[10] See R. Needham, *Belief, Language and Experience* (Oxford: Blackwell, 1972).
[11] *From Folk Psychology to Cognitive Science*, p. 229.

engaged in many superstitious speculations about the prophecies of Daniel, the apocalypse of St John, etc., does not count against the validity of his theory of motion. So by parity of reasoning the falsity of folk astronomy (if there is such a thing) should not count seriously against the validity of folk psychology.

It is pertinent to concentrate instead on the one argument of Stich's that is concerned specifically and exclusively with the concept of belief in our own culture, i.e. in the folk psychology of twentieth-century civilization, and is based on the existence of certain psychological findings. Consider, for example, an experiment of Storms and Nisbett.[12] The subjects in this experiment, whose getting-to-sleep times were all being monitored, were divided into two groups. The members of one group (the so-called 'arousal' group) were given a placebo to take fifteen minutes before going to bed and told that the pills would cause rapid heartbeat, irregular breathing, bodily warmth, and alertness, which are the typical symptoms of insomnia. The members of the other group (the 'relaxation' group) were told that the pills would have the opposite effect. The outcome was that arousal group subjects got to sleep 28 per cent faster on the nights they took the pill, while relaxation subjects took 42 per cent longer to get to sleep on the nights they took the pill. The arousal group subjects' results are explained by the experimenters as having been due to the fact that, in accordance with what attribution-theory would predict, these subjects tacitly or unconsciously 'attributed' their symptoms to the pills rather than to their own emotions and, being therefore less disturbed by the latter, got to sleep faster. Correspondingly, the relaxation group subjects' results are explained as being due to the fact that, since these subjects' symptoms persisted despite the pills, the subjects found their state of mind to be more disturbing than usual and consequently found it harder to get to sleep. But in a follow-up experiment, reported by Nisbett and Wilson,[13] the subjects speak out and tell a different story. Arousal group subjects were now told that—in the earlier experiments—they fell asleep

---

[12] M. Storms and R. Nisbett, 'Insomnia and the Attribution Process', *Journal of Personality and Social Psychology*, 2 (1970), pp. 319–23.

[13] R. Nisbett and T. Wilson, 'Talking More than We Can Know: Verbal Reports on Mental Processes', *Psychological Review*, 84 (1977). Compare K. A. Ericsson and H. A. Simon, 'Verbal Reports as Data', *Psychological Review*, 87 (1980), pp. 215–51.

faster after taking the pill, and relaxation group subjects were told that they fell asleep more slowly. And each subject was asked to report why the change in his or her sleeping-pattern took place. Arousal group subjects typically replied that they usually found it easier to get to sleep later in the week, or that they could now relax after doing well on an examination that had worried them before-hand, or that some personal problem seemed on the way to being resolved. Relaxation group subjects found similar sorts of reasons to explain their increased sleeplessness. But all *denied*—and this is crucial—that thinking about the pills was in any way responsible for what had happened to them. So the experimenters claim that in formulating their verbal reports subjects do not consult any mem-ories of the actual processes by which the changes in their sleeping-patterns came about, but tend to apply some conventional theory about what is likely to cause such changes.

Stich infers that data of this kind lend support to the view that people have two 'more or less independent cognitive systems'.[14] One of the two is largely unconscious and affects non-verbal behaviour. That is the system at work in the subjects' minds as they actually grapple with their insomnia. The other cognitive system is largely conscious and is expressed in verbal behaviour. It is the system that produces the subjects' reports about their insomnia. And Stich contrasts this dualistic thesis with the monistic assumption that he imputes to folk psychology. According to that supposed assumption, each person whose mind is made up on an issue has, at any one time, at most one cognitive attitude towards a particular resolution of the issue. Specifically, either he believes it or he disbelieves it or he has no cognitive attitude towards it. The very same belief that underlies a sincere utterance that *p* may also generate a variety of non-verbal behaviour. But, according to the supposed folk-psychological assumption, there cannot be any inconsistency at any one time between the cognitive attitude that underlies an honest and sincere utterance and the cognitive attitude underlying non-verbal behaviour that is related to the same issue. So if such an inconsistency is indeed demonstrated to exist under certain circumstances, the imputed assumption must be false. In other words, Stich argues, experimental findings like those of Storms, Nisbett, and Wilson, show that folk psychology is wrong

---

[14] *From Folk Psychology to Cognitive Science*, p. 237.

to assume a unitary cognitive system. Instead of a single system of belief it would be better to suppose 'two sub-systems of vaguely belief-like states'.[15] One of the sub-systems would interact with those parts of the mind that are responsible for verbal reporting, while the other would interact with those parts that are responsible for non-verbal behaviour. And though the two systems might often agree with one another, they might also often disagree, so that the verbal behaviour need not align itself with the non-verbal.

This argument of Stich's has been attacked by Horgan and Woodward[16] on the ground that the facts under consideration do not in fact require the existence of two separate cognitive systems. They can instead be explained, we are told, on the hypothesis of a single belief-system which sometimes operates consciously and sometimes unconsciously. Thus the subjects in the experiments described may be supposed to have believed one thing unconsciously (which they kept silent about) and something else consciously (which they reported to the experimenters). So, if one is prepared to allow the folk-psychological admissibility of unconscious belief, Stich has not made out a good case for holding that the everyday, folk-psychological concept of belief is empty.

Now there is nothing wrong with the view that unconscious belief is fully conceivable in folk psychology. As we have seen (pp. 5–7), because a belief is essentially a disposition, it may often remain unactualized and there are many reasons why this can happen. Nor is there anything wrong with the view that folk psychology may suppose an unactualized disposition to be the cause of some state of affairs. The fragility of a precious vase may cause its owner to tremble with fear when it is lifted. Instead, what is wrong with Horgan and Woodward's treatment of Stich's argument is that they assume the possibility of a person's both firmly believing and firmly disbelieving the same proposition at the same time. The proposition in question is something like: 'The cause of my worsened insomnia this week was that my emotions were more disturbing than usual, as I inferred from the fact that despite taking the relaxation pill I still had trouble getting to sleep', or 'The cause of my getting to sleep more easily this week was that my emotions

[15] Ibid. p. 231.
[16] T. Horgan and J. Woodward, 'Folk Psychology is Here to Stay', *Philosophical Review*, 94 (1985), pp. 204–11.

were less disturbing than usual, as I inferred from the fact that despite taking the arousal pill I still had little trouble getting to sleep.' There is no reason to suppose that subjects have ceased to believe one or other of these propositions unconsciously at the date at which they are asked to report why they think that their sleeping patterns have changed. So, if at that date a subject's report includes the statement that he disbelieves the proposition in question, he would indeed be ascribing to himself the firm belief that p at the same time as he has the firm belief that not-p. And the coexistence of these two beliefs is impossible. Whether or not a firm disposition is activated, it cannot belong to something that also evinces— equally strongly—the opposite disposition. A rod cannot be both reliably flexible and reliably resistant to bending, a plant cannot be both invariably hardy and invariably tender, and a person cannot both firmly believe and firmly disbelieve the same proposition at the same time. It follows that Horgan and Woodward's reply to Stich is not successful.

The right line to take against Stich is to argue, not that such a subject has flatly inconsistent beliefs, but that he *accepts* the negative of what he *believes*. That is, the subject rejects as a premiss the proposition that his symptoms were due to thinking about the pill. We have already (§3 and §12) noticed several other types of situation in which what a person accepts or rejects runs counter to what he believes or disbelieves, respectively, and this happens particularly easily in the present type of situation because the belief is an unconscious one. Moreover, there are two specific reasons why the subject here should be regarded as reporting what he accepts or rejects rather than what he believes or disbelieves. The first is that what he says is tied in with the adoption of some conventional theory or hypothesis as the premiss for his explanation. What the psychologists suppose thus is that he voluntarily chooses the type of explanation that he gives. And the second reason is that, as we have seen in §14, simple and unsophisticated belief is prior to language in a sense in which acceptance is not. Acceptance is at bottom just an interiorization of the corresponding speech-act. So it is hardly surprising if in the experiments in question belief operates without any apparent linguistic mediation, while what the subjects accept is manifest in what they report.

Finally, we must recognize that, since the difference between the concept of belief and the concept of acceptance was revealed by philosophical analysis of everyday discourse, its folk-psychological credentials are as strong as that type of analysis produces. So the source of Stich's error is his failure to do justice to the richness of the resources with which folk psychology operates. He has not noticed, or does not bear in mind, that it employs a concept of acceptance as well as a concept of belief. There is thus no need here to construct two new artificial or 'scientific' concepts of 'vaguely belief-like' cognitive systems, as he suggests should be done, since the existing folk-psychological concepts of belief and acceptance are quite adequate to the task of describing what the psychologists claim to be going on. Indeed, the conceptual apparatus of folk psychology is strikingly vindicated by its ability to accommodate experimental data of the kind that we have been considering.

Of course, it may turn out that in some cases the subjects actually believe, and do not merely accept, that their reported explanations are true. But, if this could be established, it would have to count as evidence against the alleged consequences of attribution theory. It is certainly impossible for the same person at the same time to believe firmly both that *p* and that not-*p*.

IV
Does Knowledge Imply Belief or Acceptance?

The object of scientific enquiry into the laws of nature (§16) is to obtain knowledge in the sense in which knowledge that p entails acceptance that p. But, so far as we are concerned with the experimental data that confirm or support such a theory, someone must have knowledge of them in the sense in which knowledge that p entails belief that p. The existence of these two different concepts of knowledge (§17) helps to resolve controversy about the nature of the warranty that a person must have in order to be said to know that p. Various other epistemological consequences follow (§18). In particular, it is to be noted that holism is better related to acceptance than to belief, and that philosophically induced loss of belief neither entails nor is entailed by scepticism about what is to be accepted. It has to be pointed out also (§19) that a personalist conception of the probability that p, equating it with the lowest odds accepted as being appropriate for a wager that p, should not be supposed to measure the bettor's strength of belief that p. Confirmation is available too for the view (§20) that a jury's verdict does better to declare what its members accept rather than what they believe. Furthermore it is possible (§21) to shed some light on the question whether an agent's intention to perform a certain act entails his belief that, unless prevented, he will perform that act. Attention needs also to be given (§22) to the question: when is belief a reason for acceptance? The answer to this question turns out to be closely relevant to the role of intuition in providing premisses for reasoning about moral and philosophical issues.

§16. WHAT IS THE ROLE OF BELIEF IN SCIENTIFIC ENQUIRY?

In this chapter I shall consider how the way we think about knowledge, and especially about the growth of scientific knowledge, is affected by the difference between belief and acceptance.

Knowledge that *p*, we are often told,[1] entails belief that *p*. Admittedly, as Radford showed, there is an intuitively plausible type of argument against this, which cites the possible case of someone who correctly but very hesitantly answers most of a string of questions about, say, the dates of Tudor and Stuart monarchs, so that the answerer may plausibly be said to have the relevant knowledge even though he does not really believe what he says.[2] But we can deal with Radford's type of example by asking him to tell us more about it. What would happen, we can ask, if the same questions are put to the same examinee on one or more later occasions, in circumstances where the examinee forgets what answers he gave previously and has acquired no new information that is relevant. Either the examinee gives more or less the same answers or he gives substantially different ones. If he keeps on giving more or less the same answers, that would be a good reason—other things being equal—for inferring that he did, after all, believe what he said, even if still not very confidently. It would be a good reason, that is, for inferring a disposition to feel that, for example, Elizabeth Tudor died in 1603, even though the activation of that disposition is abnormally inhibited (see §2, *Gloss no. 2*). And if the examinee gives substantially different answers that would be a good reason for inferring that he got his previous answers right only by a lucky fluke and that therefore he did not in fact have the relevant knowledge even before. In sum, the examinee either believes as well as knows or neither believes nor knows. But, though these considerations refute Radford's argument, they obviously do not establish that knowledge that *p* does indeed entail belief. They do not exclude the possibility that there may be other kinds of case in which knowledge without belief may be ascribable.

Indeed, to find such a case, we do not even have to consider degenerate cases like Radford's examinee, who is not only not a professional historian but not even a good student (since he either lacks the knowledge which he is expected to have or at least lacks any confidence that he has it). Consider instead the knowledge of physical laws that well-regarded professional scientists like

---

[1] For example, K. Lehrer, *Knowledge* (Oxford: Clarendon Press, 1974), pp. 12 and 58 f.

[2] C. Radford, 'Knowledge by Examples', *Analysis*, 27 (1966), pp. 1–11.

Einstein[3] claim explicitly to have. In such cases having the knowledge that p, where the proposition that p states a physical law, implies that the scientist accepts that p and that the proposition that p deserves acceptance in the light of cognitively relevant considerations. The scientist must be willing to go along with that proposition, and anything it is seen to entail, as a premiss—one among many—for his predictions, explanations, further research, etc. And an involuntary belief that p would not be an adequate substitute for the scientist's voluntary acceptance that p since it would not entail this policy in the choice of premisses. Nor would it deserve praise or blame in the way that a responsible act of acceptance deserves it. Perhaps there is not *much* harm done if in the end, as well as accepting that p, the scientist also believes that p. But in principle he would do better to school himself into practising a greater intellectual detachment. There is a danger that possession of a belief that p might make him less ready to change his mind about accepting that p if new evidence crops up or a better theory becomes available. It might even make him less ready to look for new evidence or a better theory, when otherwise he would have done so. Also, in the establishment of a belief that p, some factors might be influential in the black box of the scientist's subconscious mind that he would reject as irrelevant or prejudicial if they came up for consideration before the tribunal of conscious acceptance.

Ideally, therefore, a natural scientist would carry on without having any belief in the truth of his favoured hypotheses. He could rest content with accepting them in the light of cognitively relevant considerations. And any other factual investigator, such as a historian, a detective, or an intelligence analyst, could treat his own favoured hypotheses analogously. A number of distinguished philosophers have been wrong to ignore this possibility (though Descartes and Popper grasped it[4]). For example, Hume was wrong to ignore it when he supposed that all our thoughts about causal connections are beliefs[5] and are consequently, on his account of

---

[3] For example, A. Einstein and L. Infeld, *The Evolution of Physics* (Cambridge: Cambridge University Press, 1938), p. 224.

[4] R. Descartes, *The Philosophical Works*, trans. E. S. Haldane and G. R. T. Ross, vol. i (Cambridge: Cambridge University Press, 1931), 144–5 and 235–6; and K. R. Popper, *The Logic of Scientific Discovery* (London: Hutchinson, 1959), p. 46.

[5] *A Treatise of Human Nature*, bk. I, pt. III.

belief, involuntary. Correspondingly, it was wrong to hold, as Peirce did,[6] that the sole object of scientific enquiry is to put belief in the place of doubt. It is wrong to confound the analysis of inductively generated belief with that of inductively reasoned acceptance, as Harman does.[7] And it is also wrong to hold, as van Fraassen does,[8] that we have to choose between a realist analysis according to which acceptance of a scientific theory involves the belief that it is true, and an anti-realist one according to which acceptance of a scientific theory involves the belief that it is empirically adequate.

Indeed, we do not even have to treat empirical adequacy as a matter for belief and theoretical explanation as a matter for acceptance. So far from its being the case that good scientists typically seek empirically adequate knowledge of a kind that involves belief, they must be supposed rather always to seek knowledge of a kind that does not necessarily involve belief. Galileo would have remained a good scientist if he had merely accepted Copernicus's astronomy, without also believing it. Scientific enquiry, whether in pursuit of empirical uniformities or probabilities or of theoretical explanations, is not to be regarded as a procedure that is consummated only when appropriately justifiable beliefs, with novel content, arise in or come over those engaged, who have presumably been waiting patiently meanwhile for this to happen to them.

Guesses and hunches, welling up from the subconscious, may make a very considerable contribution to the progress of an enquiry. In some cases an early conviction that *p* may even usefully fortify a scientist's resolution to seek those research facilities that are necessary for testing the hypothesis that *p*, or to persevere with his experiments when he has the facilities. If he has no such conviction, he may be the kind of person who is mentally incapable of making any progress. But then, if he is convinced that *p*, his research team just as much needs other members, who do not

---

[6] C. S. Peirce, *Collected Papers*, ed. C. Hartshorne and P. Weiss (Cambridge, Mass.: Harvard University Press, 1934), v. 232. Peirce's error is mitigated by his taking what he calls 'belief' to be 'a deliberate, or self-controlled, habit' (ibid. p. 330).

[7] G. Harman, *Change in View: Principles of Reasoning* (Cambridge, Mass.: MIT Press, 1986).

[8] B. C. van Fraassen, *The Scientific Image* (Oxford: Clarendon Press, 1980), pp. 8 and 12.

believe that *p*, in order to ensure adequate open-mindedness.[9] Such members will take up appropriate attitudes towards other hypotheses. They will canvass, explore, pursue, or champion them. And in any case the culmination envisaged—the culmination that adds to our resources for explanation, prediction, technology, or further research—is a conscious and voluntary act of appropriately reasoned acceptance that is echoed throughout the relevant scientific community.

Moreover, there seem to be some quite important scientific situations in which consensual acceptance alone is appropriate and belief would be wholly out of place. A major scientific theory often encounters minor anomalies that, because no better theory is available, are taken not to justify rejecting it. Notoriously Newton's theory of motion was long in this position in relation to the movements of the planet Mercury. And the law that gives the period of oscillation of a pendulum applies only to so-called 'normal' circumstances: it does not apply where the pendulum consists of an iron ball on a string and a strong magnet has been placed under the rest position of the iron ball. So what mental attitude towards such a theory is the correct one? *Ex hypothesi* we should be wrong to believe the theory, in the sense of feeling it to be true. We cannot feel it to be a universally accurate description of the real world (though we might feel a suitably qualified version to be true). But we can accept the theory, in the sense of going along with it as a premiss, for all the purposes to which it is applicable. Certainly we might prefer a more comprehensive explanation of relevant phenomena than is at present afforded. But for the time being we accept the theory for most purposes and also accept the occasional anomalies that conflict with it.

Similarly, even when we regard a physical or chemical law as a simplification or idealization, we can use it as a premiss for predictive or explanatory calculations about the actual world, if we make relevant allowances and corrections. So in this sense we can accept the law even when we do not believe it to be true, and in fact believe it to be false, of the actual world.

Admittedly these could not be called cases of knowledge if the sense in which someone may be said to know that *p* requires it to

---

[9] See P. Kitcher, 'The Division of Cognitive Labour', *Journal of Philosophy*, 87 (1990), pp. 5–22 for further enquiry into some of the implications of this.

be actually true that *p*. But we need to look rather closely at the familiar claim (advanced by Ayer, Lehrer, Goldman, Radford,[10] and many others) that 'He knows that *p*' entails 'It is true that *p*'. What is undeniable about an ascription of knowledge that *p* is that by uttering it the utterer also implicitly admits, affirms, or otherwise commits himself to the proposition that *p*. One cannot say—literally—'He knows that *p*, and it is false that *p*.' But is this because the proposition 'He knows that *p*' entails the proposition that *p*? Or is it instead because the speech-act of saying 'He knows that *p*' normally gives the hearer to understand that the speaker is disposed to feel that *p* or has adopted the policy of premissing that *p*? We can see that the latter explanation must be the correct one when we bear in mind that the verb 'to know' may be used factively in negative or interrogative constructions[11] as well as in affirmative ones. In appropriate contexts, saying 'He does not know that *p*' or 'Does he know that *p*?' just as much commits the speaker to the implication that *p* as does saying 'He knows that *p*.' And this commitment cannot derive from an underlying entailment, because what is said is either negative or interrogative in its bearing on the issue. Moreover, since the utterance within which knowledge is ascribed may belong, as a whole, to one or other of several different kinds of speech-act, the speaker's implicit commitment to the proposition that *p* may correspondingly be an expression of belief that *p* or of acceptance that *p*.

More specifically (see §13), if the speaker states or testifies to the hearer that some third party knows that *p*, then what he implicitly expresses is his own belief that *p* (though he may also accept that *p*). But, if he asserts or acknowledges that the third party knows that *p*, then what he implicitly expresses is his own acceptance that *p* (though he may also believe that *p*). So, *pace* Cartwright,[12] it is not necessarily a lie for a scientist to claim to 'know' a law of physics that he nevertheless believes to be an idealization rather than a description of the actual world. He may mean that his policy

---

[10] A. J. Ayer, *The Problem of Knowledge* (London: Penguin, 1956), p. 35; K. Lehrer, *Knowledge* (Oxford: Clarendon Press, 1974), p. 21; A. I. Goldman, *Epistemology and Cognition* (Cambridge, Mass.: Harvard University Press, 1986), p. 19; and C. Radford, 'Belief, Acceptance and Knowledge', *Mind*, 99 (1990), p. 611.

[11] J. Lyons, *Semantics*, vol. 2 (Cambridge: Cambridge University Press, 1977), p. 599.

[12] N. Cartwright, *How the Laws of Physics Lie* (Oxford: Clarendon Press, 1983).

is to premiss it but that he lacks any disposition to feel it to be true. Equally, *pace* Radford,[13] this conception of scientific knowledge doesn't entail the possibility of scientists' having known that p, and having later come to know that q, where the proposition that p is inconsistent with the proposition that q. If you are aware of such an inconsistency and you want to assert or acknowledge that scientists now know that q, you would not—if you were rational—still say also that they knew that p, because you would not wish to declare yourself to have the policy of premissing both that p and that q.

There is yet another reason why acceptance rather than belief is a scientist's appropriate mental attitude towards his favoured theory, irrespective of any considerations about anomalies or idealizations. Philosophers have often pointed out that any general theory whatever is under-determined by any conceivable set of evidential data, as is instanced by the possibility of fitting an infinite number of different curves to any finite set of points. So in looking at the cognitively relevant considerations for choosing between two theories we may need some additional methodological criteria to supplement our evidential one. For example, we might apply appropriate criteria of conceptual simplicity, or we might have regard to the fertility of a theory in suggesting questions for further investigation. In this way we can often find cognitive, though non-evidential, reasons for accepting one out of a set of alternative theories that all cover the same evidence. We are pragmatically justified in accepting the favoured theory because our own future calculations will be made easier thereby or our research make better progress. But we are not therefore better entitled to believe in the truth of that theory than in that of any of its rivals. We should not impute our own purposes or interests to Nature. Of course, considerations of superior simplicity or fertility may in practice affect a theorist's involuntary credal feelings. But he would do well to recognize that such considerations are not justified in doing this.

What about the experimental or observational data that a scientist cites in support of accepting the theory that p? Does he need to believe that e (where the fact that e constitutes the evidential data), or only to accept that e?

---

[13] Radford, 'Belief, Acceptance and Knowledge', p. 611.

He certainly needs in any case to accept that *e*, as the premiss for the theory's inductive justification. And, if he has learned about the fact that *e* only from a reliable journal or textbook, it suffices for him merely to accept that *e*. But, so far as he himself is to be trusted as an original authority for the fact that *e* or as a putative replicator of it, he should also be taken to believe that *e* with a reasonable degree of confidence. Testimony, as we have seen (in §13), creates a presumption of such belief. Admittedly, what counts in practice as the evidential data will normally be a rich complex of methodologically structured and theoretically interpreted observations, and clearly the methodological and theoretical elements in this complex are still matters for acceptance. But the observational element requires belief on the part of whoever is either the original authority for that element or a replicator of it. Otherwise the content of scientific knowledge would be wholly a matter for human decision.

Nevertheless the law or theory that the scientist hypothesizes in order to explain the data derives its support from the data, if these are duly replicable, not from beliefs about the data. If you suppose that the existence of the scientist's beliefs about his experimental data constitutes a canonical form of support for his hypothesis, you imply that the primary task of the hypothesis is to explain or predict such beliefs. And this would have the absurd consequence of converting every science into a branch of psychology—more specifically, into a branch of the theory of belief.

Analogous points can be made about historical research, investigative journalism, police detection, military intelligence, etc. In all such cases the rock-bottom data are a matter for belief. But the enquirer needs to discover explanatory or predictive hypotheses that he can both accept himself and put forward for acceptance by others. Belief that a particular hypothesis is true may sometimes be useful in practice as a spur to the collection and examination of important evidence that would otherwise have been neglected. But it may also prejudice the enquiry or obstruct reconsideration of its results.

It may be objected that anyone who mentally accepts a theory must *believe* that it deserves acceptance, so that in the end acceptance always entails belief. But there is a *non sequitur* here. Certainly an expert who advises that such-or-such a theory is the one that best deserves acceptance gives it to be understood that this is what he believes. But a piece of advice on any subject at all gives this kind of thing to be understood. It is dishonest to offer advice to others that you do not believe to be the right advice for them. And believing that a particular generalization or prediction is the one that, at the moment, best deserves acceptance is by no means the same as believing that it is true. You might even quite consistently believe the former and disbelieve the latter (as we saw in connection with anomalies and idealizations). Or you might believe a theory to be true but disbelieve its acceptance-worthiness, perhaps because it is far too complex and inelegant. So we do not have here any reason for rejecting the overall thesis that scientific enquiry in any area should be conceived as culminating in an act of acceptance. It is just that, though the concepts of belief and acceptance are clearly enough distinct from one another, actual states of belief and acceptance in regard to connected topics are often deeply interwoven within a person's mind.

Again someone may object (as Radford has done[14]) that, if you believe a report of the relevant experimental data and believe that these data—your grounds for accepting the hypothesis—rule out any real possibility that the hypothesis is false, then you must believe also that the hypothesis is true. And that would indeed be a conceptual necessity if belief were deductively closed. But it is not (see §5). Of course it may well be that the third of these three beliefs usually accompanies the other two. But it must be rather rare for the second belief to be justified. Most of the time a wise scientist thinks of himself as accepting the best well-supported hypothesis available rather than a hypothesis that has no real possibility of being false. Such a policy is all that is normally needed, and the history of science contains many warnings against the risk of over-confidence.

Perhaps the most striking thesis, about the importance of belief in science, has been put forward by Fodor.[15] Fodor's starting-point is the fact that in many computer-run experiments the data that emerge cannot properly be regarded as experimenters' observations. So it is 'quite preposterous'[16] to assert, as Quine has done, that 'As an empiricist I continue to think of the conceptual scheme

[14] Ibid. p. 614.
[15] J. A. Fodor, 'The Dogma that Didn't Bark', *Mind*, 100 (1991), pp. 201–20.
[16] Ibid. p. 202.

of science as a tool, ultimately, for predicting future experience in the light of past experience.'[17] Instead, according to Fodor, 'What you do when you design an experiment is: you ask yourself "what outcome would make me believe that *p*; and what outcome would make me believe that not-*p*" and then you try to set things up so that you will get the first kind of outcome if and only if *p* is the case and the second kind of outcome if and only if not-*p* is the case.'[18] Or at any rate experiments are designed to increase or decrease the experimenter's degree of belief that *p* in accordance with whether or not it is the case that *p*.[19] So scientific theories, *qua* instruments, 'are calculating devices that we use to help design experimental environments in which the state of our beliefs will depend, causally, upon the state of the world'.[20] And the beliefs that matter here are those that belong to members of the relevant community: 'An experiment is at best a gadget which will induce-the-belief-that-*p* just in case it's the case that *p* in anybody rational who is *au courant* with the currently accepted theoretical framework.'[21]

Unfortunately, however, Fodor's thesis is so far from being, as he claims, 'about *how science works*'[22] that it fails to differentiate in any way between the procedures of modern experimental science and the procedures of appeal to authority as widely practised in medieval Europe. In the medieval system, enquirers had to think about which authorities to consult and how. And the actual procedure of consulting an author like Aristotle, St Paul, or Galen could equally well be said to have been designed to produce belief that *p* if and only if it was the case that *p*. You were not to doubt that your chosen authority's views expressed the truth. But you had to make sure that you understood correctly what your authority's view really was, and your textual investigations and interpretations had to cause appropriate beliefs in members of the relevant learned community.

Perhaps Fodor will reply that, so long as investigations are carried out in accordance with the theories that the contemporary scientific community respects, his account enables a sufficiently clear line to

---

[17] W. V. O. Quine, *From a Logical Point of View* (Cambridge, Mass.: Harvard University Press, 1953), p. 44.
[18] 'The Dogma that Didn't Bark', p. 211.   [19] Ibid., footnote 8.
[20] Ibid. p. 215.   [21] Ibid. p. 216.   [22] Ibid. p. 213 (Fodor's italics).

be drawn between medieval pseudo-science, on the one hand, and genuine experimental science, on the other. But such a reply would mistake the thrust of my objection. The faulty core in Fodor's account of 'how science works' is not that it fails to exclude natural pseudo-science, but that it fails to exclude appeals to reputable authority. Consulting a contemporarily respected textbook turns out, if we agree with Fodor, to be a species of experimental procedure. No distinction is drawn between doing your own research and relying on the research of others.

It is clear, therefore, that Fodor has not described conditions that suffice to pick out experimental, first-hand procedures from non-experimental, second-hand ones. Of course, his thesis about belief would still be important if it described a necessary, though not sufficient, condition that an investigation has to satisfy in order to be classifiable as experimental science. But it does not even do this.

Suppose that you have carried out an experiment designed to test whether it is the case that *p*. Then what matters is whether the result constitutes a reason for accepting that *p*, not whether it causes you to believe that *p*. If it does not constitute such a reason, then no amount of caused belief that *p* is of any cognitive value: such belief would not justify any relevant predictions or explanations. But if the result of the experiment does constitute a reason for accepting that *p*, then—at least for cognitive purposes—no belief that *p* is needed. Indeed, if it were desirable to maximize degree of belief that *p* where it is true that *p*, there are no doubt various drugs that could be used to achieve this. On Fodor's view, apparently, experimental science might make faster progress in a particular field of research if all the researchers in that field could take an appropriate credulity-enhancing drug every time they learned the outcome of each other's experiments. For what matters, on Fodor's account, is just how strongly people believe that *p* (where it is true that *p*), not how strongly they are justified in accepting that *p* (where it is true that *p*).

Perhaps Fodor would object here that my criticism is undermined by what he says about scientific theories. We use such theories, on his view, to help design experimental environments in which the state of our beliefs will depend, causally, upon the state of the world in the area of reality that is under investigation. So that would be how Fodor supposes that deviant causal chains are avoided. Strength of belief caused by the state of the world in relevant respects would mark scientific progress. Strength of belief caused—even in part—by other factors, like drugs, would not.

But now the cat is right out of the bag. Scientific theories, on Fodor's view, turn out to be a technology of belief. Their use, in the promotion of scientific research, is to enable us to generate appropriate beliefs in an appropriate way. So they are not a tool for predicting future experience in the light of past experience, as Quine claimed, or for predicting future observations in the light of past observations, as others have put the point, but a tool for predicting future beliefs in the light of past beliefs. Science as a whole is not a part of neurophysiology, as Quine's claim implied, nor is it a part of optics. Instead, Fodor implies, it is a part of cognitive psychology. But physicists are just as ill-trained for the latter as for the former, and, if Quine's claim is 'quite preposterous', so is Fodor's, or any other kind of naturalized epistemology.[23] Indeed, to characterize how experimental science works we must not only insist on its aim's being to provide justification for accepting a hypothesis rather than to cause a corresponding belief. We also need to insist on the distinctive structure of experimental justification (including its frequent reliance on already accepted theories),[24] when compared with the kind of second-hand justification that proceeds just from consulting reputable textbooks.

What is true for scientific enquiry is arguably true also for scientific education at the secondary or tertiary level. Consider any particular textbook exposition of the theory that *p*. On a long-term view the teacher's aim should not be to get students to believe that *p*, but to get them to see why—for cognitive reasons—they should accept that *p*, rather than that *q*, or that *r*, where *p*, *q*, and *r* are competing theories.

In that way the students are persuaded to accept that *p*, as an option with alternatives, instead of being caused to believe it, without any room for choice between options. They may then be considered responsible for what they think. Indeed, they thus come

[23] See also L. J. Cohen, *The Dialogue of Reason* (Oxford: Clarendon Press, 1986), pp. 41–7.
[24] As in L. J. Cohen, *The Probable and the Provable* (Oxford: Clarendon Press, 1977), pp. 129–87.

themselves to think like scientists, and in particular their minds remain open to the continuing possibility that changes may sometimes be needed in hitherto consensual scientific doctrine. And an analogous point can be made about some or all of the conclusions expounded in any other branch of intellectual education, such as mathematics, history, economics, or literary appreciation.

On the other hand, the political or religious purposes of an authoritarian society are certainly best served by teachers' seeking to indoctrinate their pupils with appropriate beliefs. Adolescents' views about abortion, for instance, may be influenced by showing them videos of aborted foetuses. And authoritarian governments may wish to stifle open-mindedness on any issue rather than to promote it, or to promulgate political or religious reasons for accepting a theory rather than cognitive ones. Such regimes have an interest thus in creating belief among the young, or acceptance for non-cognitive reasons, as well as or in place of acceptance for cognitive reasons. No doubt they will exploit the media too in order to achieve the same end with the adult populace.

Admittedly, so far as *moral* education is concerned, some good habits or recognized virtues may best be causally induced in childhood. Also in intellectual matters it may be unavoidable, or at least harmless, or even useful, for children to come to believe some of the material that they need to accept, such as basic physical laws or elementary arithmetical equations. What a free society should require is just that, at a certain level of education, children are able to experience opportunities for the acceptance or rejection of theories, principles, hypotheses, etc.

Thus, in regard to the communication of knowledge, one cannot properly understand the difference between ideals appropriate to a free society and ideals appropriate to an authoritarian one unless one keeps in mind the basic epistemological difference between acceptance and belief. But in practice few people can prevent some beliefs from creeping in even where their ideals require only acts of acceptance to occur. After all, belief is involuntary and a person can no more destroy it in himself at will than he can create it in himself at will. Complete intellectual freedom may even be too much intellectual responsibility for any mind to bear. Equally in an authoritarian regime some people may in practice resist indoctrination and exercise their innate capacity for accepting or rejecting whatever, within their own minds, they think fit. Perhaps no techniques are possible for the permanent brainwashing of a whole human community just because we have an innate potential for adopting selective policies of acceptance as well as for forming states of belief.

I grant that even under normal conditions knowledge is sometimes possible without simultaneous acceptance of what is known. Acceptance is certainly not necessary for knowledge, *pace* Popper and Lehrer.[25] Knowledge that the house is on fire can first force itself upon one's involuntary awareness when the flames begin to flicker up through the floor-boards: acceptance may, or may not, come a little later. And in a case of self-deceit a person may really know that not-*p* even though out of shame, say, or vanity he continues to premiss that *p* (see §23 below). So my claim is that, instead of saying either 'Knowledge that *p* entails acceptance that *p*' or 'Knowledge that *p* entails belief that *p*', one should prefer to say 'Knowledge that *p* entails either acceptance that *p* or belief that *p*'. Which type of knowledge is appropriate to which type of context has then to be settled separately.

It is worth noting, however, that where knowledge relies on acceptance rather than belief, it is itself subject to deductive closure, just so far as the relevant act of acceptance is thus subject. Hence, when a particular law is said to be an item of natural scientific knowledge, part of what is implied is normally that whatever is accepted to be a logical consequence of that law is also part of natural scientific knowledge. The situation in regard to mathematical knowledge, however, is rather more complex.

On what may plausibly be termed the classical view mathematical knowledge is subjectively closed under deducibility. If you know the theorem that *p*, and you are aware that the proposition that *p* entails the proposition that *q*, then you also know the theorem (or corollary) that *q*. Mathematical knowledge is thus conceived to grow by deductive extrapolation in accordance with the topic-neutral laws of formal logic. On that view, therefore, it is language-dependent, in the way in which all logical derivation is

[25] K. R. Popper, *Objective Knowledge: an Evolutionary Approach* (Oxford: Clarendon Press, 1972), pp. 24–6; and K. Lehrer, 'Belief, Acceptance and Cognition', in H. Parret (ed.), *On Believing: Epistemological and Semiotic Approaches* (Berlin: de Gruyter, 1983), pp. 173 and 180, and 'The Gettier Problem and the Analysis of Knowledge', in G. S. Pappas (ed.), *Justification and Knowledge: New Studies in Epistemology* (Dordrecht: Reidel, 1972), pp. 65–78.

language-dependent (see §14). Moreover the initial propositions, or axioms, are a matter for choice, though there may well be good reasons—consistency, completeness, etc.—for choosing some rather than others in particular contexts. So the mental attitude implicit in mathematical knowledge, when classically construed, is the attitude of acceptance.

But there is another conception of mathematical knowledge, attributable to Brouwer,[26] according to which mathematical knowledge is not extended unless some new proof-experience or subject-specific insight has occurred. The mathematician must feel intuitively that such-or-such is the way to carry out some new construction. And, though the construction itself may be voluntary, the feeling about it is not. The intuition that the mathematician has acquired is thus a kind of belief. It is therefore not even subjectively closed under deducibility (§5), and not the outcome of any linguistic convention (see §14). So on this view mathematical knowledge does not depend on logic or language for its extension, as acceptance does. And this kind of intuitionism, based as it is on an epistemological consideration, is obviously different from the kind of intuitionism, like Heyting's,[27] that relies in part on an idiosyncratic logic to differentiate it from the classical view. For even though Heyting's intuitionism rejects the law of excluded middle, it nevertheless resembles the classical view in assuming that acceptance, regulated by logic, is implicit in the extension of mathematical knowledge and that belief has no essential role in the latter.

It would, of course, be a much larger task to survey the merits and demerits of these various views of mathematical knowledge, or of other, related views. What is relevant here is just to point out that any such survey is able to draw some clarificatory analogies with the differences between belief and acceptance in non-mathematical contexts.

§17. REASONS FOR BELIEVING AND REASONS FOR ACCEPTING

Whether in science or in everyday life, there is more to its being known that *p* than just true belief or consensual acceptance.

[26] See M. Detlefsen, 'Brouwerian Intuitionism', *Mind*, 99 (1990), pp. 501–34.
[27] Ibid. pp. 525–33.

Notoriously the belief or acceptance has to be well-based. But does that mean that it has to be caused in some characteristic way or that it has to satisfy some appropriate normative criteria? I shall argue that the distinction between belief and acceptance helps to elucidate the different but interconnected roles of causal and normative reasoning in regard to the ascription of knowledge.

Clearly the kind of evidential basis that is relevant to the act of *accepting* that p is related to it normatively. The crucial point is that, since accepting that p is a voluntary act, those who seriously entertain reasons for accepting that p—whatever these reasons may be—must be in principle able *not* to accept that p. So awareness of the reasons cannot be a uniformly operative cause of their endorsement. Or, in other words, we must be able to describe a person as having taken certain facts to be reasons for accepting that p, without our thereby implying that this outcome was causally predictable from his awareness of those facts. Indeed any sufficiently counter-suggestible person will easily (by rejecting or accepting the proposition that p, respectively) refute such a causality-based prediction, if it is put to him as the supposed basis of his acceptance or rejection of the proposition that p. So, where the knowledge rests on acceptance, the basis of the knowledge must be a normative one. It needs to supply reasons why the potential knower is entitled to accept that p and would not be wrong to do so, though he is in principle able either to accept that p or not to accept that p.

But what should we say about knowledge that is conceived to rest on belief? In particular, how are beliefs warranted? Here we find a tangle of causal and normative considerations that need to be sorted out. We have to consider not only

(1) Why does George believe that it has been raining?

but also

(2) Why would it be justifiable for George to believe that it has been raining?

One appropriate answer to (1) might be

(3) There are puddles everywhere

or

(4) George has seen that there are puddles everywhere.

Now, while (3) or (4) might well be described as George's reason for accepting that it has been raining, it is clear that both (3) and (4) also point to causal factors in the situation. While (4) describes such a factor directly, (3) suggests either the same type of causal explanation as (4) or at least an explanation of George's belief by reference to the act of acceptance—taking (3) as a premiss—that caused the belief. Indeed the causal issue posed by (1) can be brought out explicitly by paraphrasing (1) as

(5) What makes George believe that it has been raining?

Yet (3) and (4) would normally do more than just provide a causal explanation of George's belief or a justification of his acceptance: they would also justify his belief. They would normally be taken to provide a reason for the belief (in the narrower sense of 'reason' in which it cannot function as a synonym for 'cause'— pp. 25–6). For, as has already been acknowledged (p. 26), we do impose standards of rationality and justifiability on our beliefs and other feeling-dispositions, despite the fact that such dispositions are involuntary and beyond our direct control. And the possibility of this normative role is confirmed when we bear in mind that (3) and (4) may constitute appropriate answers to (2) as well as to (1). As answers to (2), or equally to

(6) Why would it be justifiable for George to accept that it has been raining?,

it is clear that (3) and (4) must function as premisses in a normative argument. And, if they can thus be reasons from a prospective point of view for George's believing or accepting that it has been raining, it seems legitimate to think of them also as reasons from a retrospective point of view for this same belief. In the event, the reasons why it was justifiable for George to believe that *p* may well have been the very same reasons as those why he actually believed that *p*.

Of course, there are some cases in which reasons for accepting that *p* are not also reasons for believing that *p*. One such case (where it may not be known that *p*) is where the reasons are ethical or prudential rather than evidential or methodological, as when an advocate may have a professional reason to accept that his client is innocent, though no reason at all to believe that this is so. Another such case (where scientific knowledge would normally be reckoned to arise) is where there are sufficient experimental and simplicity-regarding reasons for accepting a scientific theory even in the face of acknowledged anomalies that constitute good reasons for not feeling the theory to be true in all its implications. A third such case (where scientific knowledge also arises) is where the choice between various theories is underdetermined by the evidence and the reasons for accepting one of them are partly methodological—for example, superior simplicity to its rivals. Nevertheless, even though questions like (6) will not always have the same answers as questions like (5), any reason for believing that *p* is also a reason for accepting that *p*. So any case of human knowledge involving belief is in principle transformable—by a decision of the believer—into a case of knowledge involving acceptance.

An apparent exception to this occurs when belief is said to have been brought about in some non-rational manner, as when perhaps a televiewer is said to have come to believe that *p* because of his channel's broadcasting—unknown to the public—frequent subliminal repetitions of the statement that *p*. If that channel were said to be allowed to engage in subliminal advertising only when the text of the advertisement is a true one, the belief certainly could be said to have been induced by a reliable process—a process that can be relied on to produce only true beliefs. And, if beliefs so induced were indeed adequately based, it looks as though we would have here an example of knowledge in which the belief is not related normatively to its basis and so no transformation into a case of knowledge involving acceptance is possible.

Admittedly this situation, if indeed it ever exists anywhere, would be one in which the supposed knower would have nothing whatever to say in answer to the question 'How do you know that *p*?' He could neither justify nor explain his belief that *p*. Nor would he have just forgotten who gave him the information that *p*: he was never even aware of having been given that information. Nevertheless, the nature of the belief's origin does in fact justify it. The supposed reliability of the subliminally advertised message provides a perfectly adequate justification for the belief. It is just that the existence of this justification is unknown to the believer. In other words he knows without knowing that he knows.

§18. SOME EPISTEMOLOGICAL COROLLARIES

In the development of knowledge, as we have seen in §17, rationality exercises pressure on both belief and acceptance, though not in all the same ways. Let us examine some of the consequences of this.

First, a significant constraint is imposed on measures of inductive or evidential support. If acceptance of a proposition is held to be justified only if the level of support for the proposition reaches at least as high as some canonical threshold, we must bear in mind the implications of taking acceptance to be deductively closed (§5). If every proposition deducible from an accepted proposition, in accordance with accepted rules, is also accepted, as subjective deductive closure requires, it follows that every proposition deducible, according to accepted rules, from a proposition that has canonical support must also have at least canonical-level support. And this requirement will exclude certain types of support-measure from being applicable. For example, no canonical threshold of prior improbability may be judged requisite for the acceptance of a hypothesis that survives testing, since where H_1 entails H_2 it is possible for the improbability of H_2 to be less than that of H_1. That is, a Popper-type[28] measure of support in terms of prior improbability does not ensure that canonical-level support is transmitted by entailment. Hence, if we use it to determine a threshold for acceptance, it gives us no guarantee that what would normally be accepted to be the deductive consequences of acceptable hypotheses will also qualify for acceptance. If science aims at the acceptance of well-supported theories rather than at belief in them, a Popper-type measure of support is inappropriate. So too is a measure in terms of the excess of posterior over prior probability, since that measure also does not ensure that canonical-level support is transmitted by entailment. But a measure in terms of posterior probability *simpliciter* does not fail in this respect, nor does a measure in terms of Baconian induction.[29]

Secondly, it is acceptance, not belief, that is properly subject, from an epistemological point of view, to holistic constraints. Whether or not it is right to add the proposition that p to, retain it in, or remove it from, our set of potential premisses in a particular context of reasoning, is a question that may in principle depend for its answer on the whole existing membership of that set. Ideally it

---

[28] Popper, *The Logic of Scientific Discovery*, pp. 251–76 and 387–419, esp. 391.

[29] See L. Jonathan Cohen, *An Introduction to the Philosophy of Induction and Probability* (Oxford: Clarendon Press, 1989), pp. 139 and 162.

is unsatisfactory to add or retain a premiss that is inconsistent with some existing premisses: one or more premisses must be excluded so as to maintain consistency. And one has to bear in mind here— in relation to the possibility of inconsistencies—not only the new premiss itself but also all the consequences that may follow from the conjunction of that premiss with one or more existing premisses. Of course, a new premiss of this kind is commonly accepted in certain circumstances, as when a new scientific theory is accepted in the face of anomalies that conflict with it (§16). But when that occurs it would be an acknowledged imperfection, the need for which would be eliminated by the construction of a better theory.

The rationality of belief, however, is a very different matter. Since beliefs are not deductively closed, they cannot be intrinsically subject to any holistic requirement for overall consistency (as we saw in §6). And at the heart of this willingness to tolerate inconsistencies of belief, in certain cases, is the implicit awareness that belief is involuntary. Because a person's amalgam of beliefs, like his medley of desires, is outside his own direct choice, it is not as appropriate a subject-matter for holistic evaluations of rationality as is his system of accepted premisses, his system of adopted goals, or their combination. So far as a mental state is involuntary, and not eliminable by any voluntary action, no laudability or culpability belongs to being in it, and where there is no laudability in consistency, nor culpability in inconsistency, evaluations of rationality lose their bite.

Again, you may decide to systematize, or even to axiomatize, what you accept in a particular type of context, in order to spot inconsistencies and have appropriate premisses readily available when needed. And it may also be important to do the same for your goals in order to facilitate their achievement. But if your beliefs or desires are systematized at all it happens involuntarily. Holism is a policy for acceptance, not for belief—though what you accept may have a big impact on what you believe.

There is a corollary here for applications of the so-called 'principle of charity'. If you are trying to discover how another person actually does think (as distinct from assessing how you or he ought to think), you may think it right to assume on each issue, in default of specific evidence to the contrary, that he is fully consistent, in order to be able to draw holistic inferences from what you do know about him. But this assumption is more appropriately applied to the study of what premisses a person accepts, or of what goals he adopts, than to the study of what he believes or desires. Charity is the alternative to censure and is therefore pertinent, as censure is, only where error is voluntary. Beliefs and desires crop up involuntarily in such unpredictable ways, without even subjectively computed deductive closure, that it is often more appropriate to treat them atomistically than holistically.

Thirdly, there are some implications here for the characterization and critique of scepticism. In one familiar form the epistemological sceptic is presented as a person who argues—in relation to any particular claim to know that p—that you can never know either that there is conclusive proof for the proposition that p or that the process inducing your thought that p is a fully reliable one. You offer what seem to be veritable paradigms of warranted certainty, as when a person thinks he knows that his hand is in front of his face because he sees it there and touches it with his nose. But the sceptic comes up in each case with outlandish possibilities which refute your paradigm, such as the possibility that an evil neurologist is inducing illusions in you. So your confidence in your paradigms is shattered and you are tempted to admit that, even if you were in fact to know that p, you could never know that you knew. Hence it is apparently right to be sceptical about the existence of knowledge despite the fact that people often claim to have it.

However, careful attention to the difference between belief and acceptance enables us to see this situation in a clearer light, so that the paradox becomes resoluble. Your belief in the conclusive provability of the proposition that p may indeed be gravely weakened by your consideration of the sceptic's argument. You may even lose your disposition to feel that the process inducing your thought that p is a reliable one. But loss of belief here does not entail cessation of acceptance. You may continue with the policy of premising that it is conclusively provable that p even if you no longer have the corresponding belief. And there may be good cognitive reasons for this continuance, such as that the counter-arguments are too outlandish to take seriously whereas the supporting arguments are solid and respectable.

What emerges, therefore, is that, though the sceptic may persuade some people that they have no belief-based knowledge that knowledge exists, they can still have acceptance-based knowledge that it does. And the existence of the latter kind of knowledge is not touched by the sceptic's mode of argumentation.

In another and even more iconoclastic form the epistemological sceptic is presented as a person who argues that there is never any reason to believe anything, so knowledge is impossible: he cannot know that he is not dreaming, that his physical environment is as it is seen to be, that his fire is the cause of his feeling warm, and so on. 'Our senses certainly suffer sometimes from illusion,' the sceptic may be supposed to say, for example, 'so perhaps they always do.' It is then objected that by offering such arguments in favour of his philosophical claims the sceptic implicitly admits the existence of some beliefs for which good reasons exist, namely philosophical beliefs, and thereby contradicts his own claim that any knowledge is impossible. But if belief and acceptance are adequately distinguished from one another the sceptic may adopt a more tenable position. What he certainly queries are the reasons for believing anything to be as it appears to be. But he can present his own philosophical thesis as an accepted or acceptance-worthy premiss rather than as a belief. Correspondingly, he can claim that people may accept, though they would be irrational to believe, what they are told by others about the irrationality of their beliefs. There is therefore a point in his giving voice to certain remarks about his own philosophy: he might thereby persuade others to accept and propagate it. They would not be justified in feeling it to be true, but might be justified in taking it as a premiss for their own reasonings. That is not to say that this scepticism about belief-worthiness is correct. It may well be open to other kinds of criticism than the charge of self-refutation that is discounted here. But at least it can be coherently propounded.

Moreover, an opposite kind of scepticism might advocate the pointlessness of all proof, reasoning, or deliberation. On this view it would be acceptance, not belief, that was intrinsically irrational. And the sceptic would then have to avoid claiming or urging acceptance of his thesis. But he might nevertheless hope to cause others to share his belief in its truth. What a sceptical epistemology cannot coherently propound is the irrationality of both belief and acceptance.

Fourthly, the distinction between belief and acceptance also has some implications for the roles of faith and natural theology, respectively, in the search for what might count as religious knowledge. In the sense of 'reliance' or 'trust', faith is clearly a voluntary activity. You may decide, for example, to have faith in God's mercy as well as in your stockbroker's recommendations. But in the other everyday sense of 'faith' (as distinct from any special use given the term by particular religious doctrines[30]), faith that God exists is involuntary—an example of belief, not of acceptance. In this sense faith is just religious belief.[31] Indeed, people sometimes regret that they have lost their faith. So it is certainly not a state of mind that can be directly achieved, restored, or maintained by an immediately operative decision, though people often try hard to induce it in themselves or in others or hope that God will so induce it. Of course, the bare acceptance of certain propositions about God, about religious rituals, or about the immortality of human souls, is sometimes said to be capable eventually of bringing faith into being (p. 18). But religious faith is not to be confused with unreasoned or inadequately reasoned acceptance, even though it may be promoted by this. Again, faith that God exists is often said to take the place of a proof that God exists. But what it actually replaces is the mental act of acceptance in the light of such a proof. Roughly speaking, we can say that a religion of faith stands to natural theology as belief to reasoned acceptance.

§19. WHAT HAS SUBJECTIVE PROBABILITY TO DO WITH
STRENGTH OF BELIEF?

The distinction between belief and acceptance has no special impact on objectivist analyses of probability. The existence of such-and-such a relative frequency, say, or of such-and-such a causal propensity is a matter of fact towards which, like other matters of fact, either a passive or an active attitude of cognition may be exercised. You can either believe, or accept, or both believe and

---

[30] See, for example, A. Broadie, *Notion and Object: Aspects of Late medieval Epistemology* (Oxford: Clarendon Press, 1989), p. 173: 'Almost every Medieval theologian asserts that faith is by an act of will.' William James, *The Will to Believe and Other Essays in Popular Philosophy* (New York: Longmans Green, 1901), pp. 1–31 makes the same assertion about what he calls 'belief' that God exists. But what he says fits acceptance, not belief.

[31] See, for example, J. B. Sykes (ed.), *The Concise Oxford Dictionary of Current English*, 6th edn. (Oxford: Clarendon Press, 1976), p. 373.

accept, that the probability of a bank-cashier's being a feminist is 0.2, for example, if by 'probability' here you mean relative frequency or causal propensity.

But suppose that you are a personalist, subjectivist, or Bayesian. Suppose you hold, accordingly, that a spoken or written assessment of probability is to be understood as describing or avowing some feature of the assessor's own state of mind. You need then to ask: is that feature to be identified with a passive or an active attitude of cognition? Frank Ramsey, for example, explicitly identified a person's assessment of the probability that p with a declaration of his or her degree of belief that p.[32] De Finetti has held a similar view.[33] And in taking this line Ramsey and de Finetti have been followed by most subjectivists, including the authors of the latest Bayesian text, Howson and Urbach.[34] But is such a view just a Humean, positivist prejudice—a historically accidental accretion —which a sophisticated neo-Cartesian subjectivism could discard? Could there be an acceptance-based subjectivism? Or is reference to belief a necessary feature of any attempt to analyse assessments of probability as declarations about features of the assessor's own state of mind?

In considering how a subjectivist point of view can best be formulated, it is clearly material to consider first how belief can be measured. Ramsey himself argued against the view that by 'degree of belief' we mean the intensity of the feeling that accompanies a belief. 'The beliefs which we hold most strongly', he said, 'are often accompanied by practically no feeling at all; no one feels strongly about things he takes for granted.'[35] But this argument is a *non-sequitur*. Taking for granted is a form of acceptance, not of belief. And, even if it were not, Ramsey's argument would at best concern the feelings that *accompany* the activation of a belief, not the feelings that constitute it. When you take it for granted that p, you

---

[32] F. P. Ramsey, *The Foundation of Mathematics* (London: Routledge and Kegan Paul, 1931), pp. 159–90.

[33] B. de Finetti, 'Foresight: Its Logical Laws, Its Subjective Sources (1937)', in H. E. Kyburg and H. E. Smokler (eds.), *Studies in Subjective Probability* (New York: John Wiley and Sons, 1964), pp. 99–158. See also B. de Finetti, *Theory of Probability: A Critical and Introductory Treatment*, trans. A. Machi and A. Smith (London: John Wiley, 1974), p. 3.

[34] C. Howson and P. Urbach, *Scientific Reasoning: The Bayesian Approach* (La Salle: Open Court, 1989), pp. 56–63.

[35] *The Foundations of Mathematics*, p. 169.

are disposed to have a strong feeling that *p* if the occasion arises for an activation of that disposition. But in so far as you take it for granted that *p* you tend not to let such an occasion arise. Indeed, if you were to say that you are *not* disposed to have a strong feeling that *p*, people would infer that you had only middling or weak feelings that *p* and therefore that you were correspondingly unlikely to take it for granted that *p*.

Ramsey's own view about the measurement of belief was that people reveal their assessments of the probability that *p* by the lowest odds on which they will bet that *p*. In fact, according to Ramsey, 'a person's actions are completely determined by his desires and opinions',[36] where 'opinion' is a synonym for 'belief'. So, according to Ramsey, the action of placing a bet at certain odds is to be explained in terms of the bettor's desire for the goods that are at stake in the bet and the strength of the bettor's belief about the outcome. Indeed Ramsey thinks that strength of belief that *p* is hardly to be known otherwise than via the believer's lowest odds for betting that *p*.

But we have seen earlier (§§7–12) that there is also a quite different way of explaining a person's behaviour, whether the behaviour be concerned with bets or with anything else. Specifically, some of a person's behaviour may have a rational explanation—an explanation in terms of the premisses that he accepts and the goals that he adopts. So an alternative basis for subjectivism would be to reject any concern with the measurement of belief, whether conceived as intensity of feeling or as lowest betting odds, and to build instead on the assumption that a person's betting behaviour is most appropriately explained by the premisses that he accepts and the goals that he adopts. That assumption has quite a number of advantages over Ramsey's method of explaining betting behaviour.

First, it allows for the possibility of insincerity. This is important because a person's betting behaviour can be designed to conceal his real belief about the outcome rather than to reveal it.

A second point that has relevant implications for subjectivism is the importance—in science—of accepting a theory rather than believing it (see §16 above). Subjectivists are normally Bayesians in their methodology for science, measuring evidential confirmation

---

[36] Ibid. p. 173.

for a theory by the extent to which the posterior probability of the theory on the evidence exceeds the theory's prior probability. That posterior probability is thus treated as a highly relevant considera-tion in determining whether or not the theory should be accepted. But, if a scientist who accepts the theory that p does best to lack any belief that p (as argued in §16), his personal evaluation of the posterior probability that p should not amount to a declaration of his degree of belief that p. For, if it does, the acceptance-worthiness of the theory is made to depend, at least in part, on the strength of his belief that the theory is true. In sum, the view that in science, and other intellectual enquiry, acceptance rather than belief is the right attitude to have towards a preferred theory carries with it the view that the probability of the theory should not be construed in terms of partial belief.

A third way in which the distinction between belief and accept-ance affects the subjectivist conception of probability is that it engages quite sharply with the issue of coherence. Since wagers are voluntary undertakings, which do not necessarily reflect the strength or weakness of the bettor's underlying mental feelings, the bettor's offer of his lowest odds on the proposition that p claims to reflect what he accepts in his mind as being appropriate about the terms on which he will bet rather than to reflect the strength or weakness of his underlying mental feelings. And it would not be possible to set up a rational methodology for assessing probabilities on the basis of such subjectively assigned betting-odds unless the requisite coherence of such assignments—i.e. their resistance to a Dutch book (in which the bettor loses money overall whatever the outcomes)—were conceived in terms of coherent acts of acceptance rather than of coherent states of belief. Coherence, in this context, has to be an attainable norm. Otherwise the process involving it could hardly be the concern of a methodology. And, if coherence is to be an attainable norm, the attitudes required for it must be within a person's voluntary powers to achieve, as beliefs are not. So, whatever Bayesians *say* about strength of belief, what their methodology must actually operate with is acceptance. The strength of a person's various interrelated beliefs may in fact be distributed quite rationally. But, if so, he may just be lucky. What Bayesian methodologists can recommend him to ensure is that his *accepted* betting odds cohere when he originates or revises them.

Of course, certain beliefs are indeed relevant here. On a subjectivist view one legitimate reason for a person's accepting such-or-such odds for betting that *p*—if he can do so coherently—may be because he has such-or-such a strength of belief that *p*. The subjectivist thesis is then, in effect, that in these circumstances the belief may justify the acceptance: its occurrence is a cognitively relevant consideration. But to say this is not to imply that the strength of a person's belief that *p* actually constitutes his evaluation of the probability that *p*. What justifies a particular cognitive attitude cannot be identical with what constitutes it. That becomes very clear where what justifies your acceptance of such-and-such odds on its being true that *p* is not the strength of your belief that *p* but some cognitively irrelevant factor, such as your aim to attract others to bet with you on the issue.

A fourth point here concerns the monitoring of biases. If personal probabilities are held to be constituted by acceptance, not belief, people are encouraged to take a more active view of how these probabilities should be evaluated. No doubt one piece of evidence that a person should take into account in any such evaluation, as already remarked, is the strength of his own passive feeling of confidence in the relevant outcome. Treating his belief-system—i.e. the causal system generating his belief—as a black box, he is entitled to record the content and strength of its output when available information is fed into it. He may indeed form a provisional assessment of appropriate odds on this basis. But if he is prudent he will adjust this provisional assessment in the light of what he believes about his own biases, such as tendencies towards over-confidence or under-confidence in certain kinds of outcome. That is to say, he might take those beliefs as reasons for accepting in the end an assessment of subjective probability that differs somewhat from the assessment that the black-box procedure on its own would generate. So, by making acceptance crucial, rather than belief, we allow room for him to exercise conscious self-control, even prior to ensuring coherence. And then, because acceptance is voluntary, people can be considered responsible for inadequacies of self-correction in their fundamental assessments. Indeed, so long as subjective probability is supposed to be rooted in involuntary degree of belief, a subjectivist analysis is unsuitable for any situations in which a person, like a weather-forecaster or a market-analyst, may be held culpable for his or her assessments of probability. But people can be held accountable for probability-assessments made in subjective terms, if instead what is ultimately crucial is what they accept.

The distinction between belief and acceptance pays yet another dividend in this context. It undermines van Fraassen's recent argument for the voluntariness of belief.[37]

Van Fraassen begins by arguing that someone operating over time with a subjectivist, Ramsey-type conception of probability would avoid a Dutch book's being made against him only on one or other of two conditions. One of the two possible conditions is that the person concerned has no beliefs about the reliability of his own future judgements. The other is that he has a degree of present belief n about a certain future outcome on the supposition that he will in the future have a degree of belief m about that outcome, if and only if $n = m$. The former of these two conditions would normally be too restrictive to be admissible. So, van Fraassen argues, the second condition has to be satisfied. And the only way to reconcile oneself to this is to see the latter condition as a form of commitment to stand behind one's own commitments. Consequently, since commitments have to be undertaken voluntarily, we need to look on any commitment-carrying gradations of subjective probability as also being voluntary. And if such gradations are gradations of belief, concludes van Fraassen, then belief itself must be voluntary.

However, van Fraassen's argument clearly collapses if the gradation of personal probability that p has in any case to be treated as a gradation of the lowest accepted odds that p and not as a gradation of strength of belief that p. Van Fraassen's two conditions for avoiding a diachronic Dutch book must then be reformulated in terms of acceptance, which is admittedly voluntary, and no conclusions can be drawn from either of them about the nature of belief. Indeed, when appropriately reformulated the argument must rather be taken to reinforce the thesis that any subjectivist measure of probability must be related to acceptance, not belief. That is to say, if belief is indeed involuntary—as there are other good reasons to suppose (§4)—van Fraassen's reasoning may be viewed as a *reductio ad absurdum* proof for the thesis that the degree of a person's subjective probability that p should be

[37] B. van Fraassen, 'Belief and the Will', *Journal of Philosophy*, 81 (1984), pp. 235–56.

identified not with his degree of belief that *p*, but with his accepted assessment of the lowest odds for betting that *p*.

My reasoning here is not directed towards defending subjectivism against the arguments of those who advocate objectivist accounts of probability—relative frequency analyses, propensity analyses, and so on. I am not even taking the opportunity to champion the pluralist account that I myself prefer.[38] Instead my point is just that, *if* the subjectivist option is to be stated, its statement should discard any reference to degree of belief and take acceptance to be the mental attitude that is crucially involved. In this way, I have argued, we provide an appropriately rational explanation for a person's betting behaviour, we treat that behaviour as voluntary and capable of insincerity, we fit in with the cognitive attitude that it is appropriate to adopt towards a preferred scientific theory, we leave room for methodological promptings and attributions of responsibility that are aimed at the pursuit of coherence and the avoidance of bias, and we can escape a diachronic Dutch book without committing ourselves to the paradoxical doctrine that belief is voluntary.

An important point to notice, however, is that we do not then just replace the term 'belief' in the conventional personalist analysis by the term 'acceptance'. The issue is not a merely verbal one. Though acceptance, like belief, may vary with the occasion, it is unlike belief in not being able to vary in degree. A person may take the proposition that *p* as a premiss for business purposes but not in his private life, just as his belief that *p* may come and go with the presence or absence of some persuasive informant. But acceptance does not admit of any other kind of internal variation than in its content. Of course, acceptance-worthiness is a matter of degree. But it is not a subjective state of mind, like degree of belief. Also, a person's inclination to take the proposition that *p* as his premiss may be stronger than his inclination so to take the proposition that *q*. But inclinations are prior to decisions or the formation of intentions, while acceptance that *p* ensues upon, and executes, a decision or an intention to accept that *p*. Acceptance that *p* cannot therefore itself be stronger than acceptance that *q* in the way that a person's inclination to accept that *p* may be stronger than his

[38] Cohen, *An Introduction to the Philosophy of Induction and Probability*, pp. 40–114.

inclination to accept that *q*. To accept that *p* is to adopt the policy of taking the proposition that *p* as a premiss in appropriate circumstances, and you either adopt that policy or you don't. That is why philosophers of science have argued about the level of a theory's probability, confirmation, support, etc. that may be appropriate for the theory's acceptance. Probability, confirmation, support, etc. are matters of degree in terms of which, alongside other considerations, scientists may be able to fix a threshold of acceptance for the theory. In contrast, it is because beliefs are dispositions to have certain feelings that they can vary in strength with the intensity of those feelings. Indeed, the variation in possible intensity of belief-feelings from mere suspicion to overwhelming conviction is obviously comparable with such other variations of feeling as that from mere irritation to overwhelming fury, from slight unease to panic terror, or from gentle satisfaction to fierce exultation. So failure to distinguish adequately between belief and acceptance is bound to lead to confused disagreements, like that of Newman with Locke about whether there are degrees of 'assent'.[39]

It follows that, when the probability that *p* is measured by the lowest odds at which a person is prepared to bet that *p*, we have to think of the parameter of probability that is thus measured as a gradation of something that the person accepts about the proposition that *p* rather than as a gradation of his acceptance that *p*. You can perhaps first accept that it is appropriate for you to bet only on rather long odds that *p*, and later accept that it is appropriate for you to bet on shorter odds. But what thus changes in degree is the length of odds that you accept, not your own act of acceptance.

Moreover, this attribution of change to the object of gradation has important consequences for the complementationality of the resultant function. According to the laws of the mathematical calculus of chance, if the probability that *p* is very nearly minimal, the probability of not-*p* has to be very nearly maximal. But if a person's belief that *p* is so weak as to be almost non-existent, it certainly does not follow necessarily that he has a very strong belief that not-*p*. There might be just a very little evidence to sway him either way. So the degree-of-belief account of subjective probability tends to clash with the complementational principle for the proba-

---

[39] See H. H. Price, *Belief* (London: Allen and Unwin, 1969), pp. 130–56.

bility of a negation. An account in terms of acceptance, however, does not face any difficulty here. To accept that it is appropriate for you to bet on long odds that p is necessarily equivalent to accepting that it is appropriate for you to bet on short odds that not-p.

Of course, just as you can accept that certain odds are the right ones, so too you can believe this. But that has nothing to do with the gradation of belief—only with the gradation of odds.

There is a tempting objection, however, that runs roughly as follows. 'One must agree that willingness to wager at not lower than such-or-such odds is a poor measure of a person's disposition to feel confident that p. Like any other analysis of a mental state in terms of a supposedly equivalent behavioural readiness, this measure falls foul of the possibility of pretence. It is always possible to make bets that will deceive people about what you really believe. But this difficulty is easily dodged if one replaces the behavioural analysis by a corresponding intellectual one. The strength of a person's belief that p is now to be measured by the odds that he believes to be appropriate between any punter and any bookmaker for a bet that p, whether or not he is actually willing or able to make such a bet. It is thus quite unnecessary to introduce the concept of acceptance into one's characterization of the situation.'

But presumably belief in the appropriateness of something can itself vary in strength. So a question arises about how such a belief is to be measured. And there is a dilemma here. Either we are to measure this belief in the same way as that in which we are able to measure all the believer's other beliefs, in which case we shall have to find out what he believes to be an appropriate wager on the appropriateness of his first wager, and so on, so that the proposed criterion of probability gets caught up in an infinite regress and lacks effectiveness. Or alternatively we are to judge strength of belief in the appropriateness of a wager by some other criterion, and the question then arises why we could not have just used that criterion in the first place. We can, however, escape through the horns of this dilemma, and avoid any problem about pretence, by taking a person's subjective probability to be measured by the odds that he accepts for cognitively relevant considerations, rather than by the strength of belief which may or may not accompany that acceptance. Since acceptance is not a matter of degree, the regress cannot get started.

§20. SHOULD A JURY'S VERDICT DECLARE WHAT ITS
MEMBERS BELIEVE OR WHAT THEY ACCEPT?

In different lawcourts issues of fact are decided in different ways. In some they are decided by a single legally trained judge, in some by a panel of judges, in some by one or more judges afforced by one or more technically expert assessors, and in some by a specified number of lay jurors. But what does such a trier of fact properly give the world to understand when he, she, or they announce a verdict against the defendant? Do jurors imply in a criminal case, for example, that they are disposed to have a feeling of conviction that the defendant is guilty? Or do they imply that the court should adopt a policy of premissing that this is so? Are they claiming that they have been uncontrollably overwhelmed by a belief? Or are they declaring that they treat the evidence and arguments put before them as adequate reason for accepting that the defendant is provably guilty?

The point is not an unimportant one, because considerations of belief and considerations of acceptance may lead in different directions. For example, a juror, because of some racial prejudice that he is powerless to discard, may experience a deep and unalterable feeling of conviction that the defendant has been proved guilty. Yet, if he carefully evaluates the strength of the evidence before the court, he may think it reasonable for him to reject that proposition. Or he may firmly believe that the defendant has been proved guilty but be unwilling to accept that he should convict because he deems the law under which the defendant is being tried to be unjust. Or he may believe that a key witness for the defence is lying, but be incapable of giving any other reasons than this belief for accepting that the witness is lying, so he hesitates to accept that proposition even though he believes it. Or, on the other hand, he may be willing to accept what follows in the instant case from some rule of evidence—such as a presumption of guilty knowledge or a requirement for corroboration—but be quite unable to have the corresponding belief or absence of belief.

Actually there is a threefold issue here.

One kind of question is about how different legal systems require their triers of fact to operate. For example, so far as English criminal courts are concerned, was Lord Diplock right in *Henry*

Walters v. *The Queen* to approve of Lord Goddard's statement in *R.* v. *Kritz* that the judge should make the jury understand that 'they have to be satisfied and must not return a verdict against a defendant unless they feel sure'?[40] And was Sir Owen Dixon right to say in the Australian case of *Briginshaw* v. *Briginshaw*: 'The truth is that, when the law requires the proof of any fact, the tribunal must feel an actual persuasion of its occurrence or existence before it can be found. It cannot be found as a result of a mere mechanical comparison of probabilities independently of any belief in its reality.'[41] If those distinguished judges were right, the English and Australian systems certainly require a convicting jury to *believe* that the defendant's guilt has been proved beyond reasonable doubt, whether or not it also *accepts* that proposition. On the other hand, the old Carolingian code, with its exact proof-metric, clearly laid down conditions under which the guilt of an accused had to be accepted whether or not the judges believed it, such as when there were adequate grounds for torture and a confession was extracted.[42] But these are questions about actual legal systems and outside the scope of our present enquiry.

A second kind of question that arises here concerns the ways in which triers of fact operate in practice, whether or not these patterns of operation conform to the relevant legal requirements. And about such questions there is obviously room for sociological or psychological enquiry, which again is outside our present concern.

But there is a third kind of question here, and one that has a more philosophical orientation. Existing rules and practices may not be ideal, or even consistent. So we can ask also: what does justice, or the public good, require? Or, if such an unqualified question is too simplistic, we can ask instead: what conditions are relevant here to the requirements of justice, the public good, etc. with respect to the belief/acceptance issue? Should belief that it has

---

[40] Quoted in R. Eggleston, *Evidence, Proof and Probability*, 2nd edn. (London: Weidenfeld and Nicolson, 1983), p. 117: see [1969] 2 App. Cas. 26, 30 (PC 1968) (Jamaica), and [1950] 1 KB 82, 89 (1949), respectively. The English court of criminal appeal has ruled to this effect; see G. Williams, *The Proof of Guilt*, 3rd edn. (London: Stevens, 1963), p. 191.

[41] Ibid. pp. 132–3: see 60 CLR 361 (Austl. 1938).

[42] See J. H. Langbein, *Prosecuting Crime in the Renaissance: England, Germany, France* (Cambridge, Mass.: Harvard University Press, 1974), pp. 259 ff.

been proved that p be sufficient for a verdict that p? Should it even be necessary for such a verdict?

It is easy to see why the present state of English and Australian law, as viewed by Diplock, Goddard, and Dixon, could seem satisfactory in relevant respects. In the English and Australian jury systems a group of people recruited from the populace at large has no other function to perform than the delivery of a verdict on the facts presented to it. Such a lay jury, from the point of view of the general public, normally operates rather like what psychologists call a black box. It receives an input of data from the testimony and behaviour of witnesses, from advocates' arguments, from judicial notice, statements of law, and summing-up, etc. It delivers an apparently non-random output in the form of a verdict. But it discloses nothing then about the intervening process, except whether or not the verdict is unanimous. Neither the jury as a whole nor its individual members pronounce any reasons for the verdict, and individual jurors are discouraged from describing later what happened during their deliberations. Any appeal on a factual issue or any declaration of a mistrial, has therefore to be grounded on defects in the evidence, procedure, or summing-up rather than on identifiable pieces of mistaken reasoning by the jury. So on the information officially available all one can say is that, in the circumstances present, what is put into the black box somehow determines its output. The relation between input and output can thus be treated as a causal one. But there is certainly no official ground for supposing that any reasoning at all has taken place, let alone that the reasoning has had this or that specific structure (except perhaps in so far as the judge may have been consulted about some point of law or fact that has arisen during the jury's deliberations, or the jury may have been asked to give 'special verdicts' on some particular issues). Hence one might well think that there is no point in setting up legal rules about how a jury should deliberate: such rules would not be enforceable by the court. Any institutional safeguard against the influence of illegitimate considerations—intimidation, corruption, racial, religious, or sexist bias, emotional susceptibility, gossip, popular superstition, prejudgement by the media, etc.—must lie in the surveillance of individual jurors, or in the size and composition of the jury or of its requisite majority. Accordingly, because belief is explicable in terms of causation and acceptance is explicable in terms of reasoning (§§7–12), such a system seems to favour the view that a jury's verdict expresses what they (or a permissible majority of them) believe rather than what they accept. And within this kind of institutional framework it is quite intelligible why some professional judges may come to hold it just that conviction, or feeling sure, should constitute the requisite warranty for a jury's verdict of guilt. Indeed, it may also be much easier for lay jurors to introspect their own feelings than consciously to compute the validity of proofs.

However, the black-box character of the jury's deliberations is not the only factor to affect the issue, even if we were to confine our attention to the Common Law tradition.

Obviously another important factor here is the tendency of juries to reflect the prevailing values of their community in their decisions. If the penalty that would follow conviction is seen as being too severe, or if the alleged crime is regarded, in the circumstances, as an honourable deed or a public service, a jury may give a verdict of acquittal despite strong evidence of guilt. What is happening then? You may be tempted to say that in pronouncing their verdict the jurors purport to believe that the defendant has not been proved guilty, while they actually believe that he has. But that description of the situation does impute deliberate dishonesty or deception to the jurors. Such an imputation may sometimes be correct. But normally no one is deceived about the jurors' actual state of mind in such cases, so it seems wrong to describe their state of mind in terms that imply dishonesty. Indeed a juror certainly need not think of himself as being dishonest in this way if the correct description of his conduct is to say instead that he deems the defendant not to have been proved guilty, and accordingly acquits him, while nevertheless believing him to have been proved guilty. Jurors would then be accepting on ethical or pragmatic grounds, rather than on cognitive ones, that the accused is not guilty, while believing, perhaps quite firmly, in his or her guilt. So the verdict would declare what the jury accepts, not what it believes. Of course, in many, if not most, jurisdictions this kind of behaviour conflicts with a jury's formal obligations. But the fact that—in suitable circumstances—a jury is likely to behave like this is a major reason for the continued popularity of the jury system. Correspondingly that popularity tends not to sit so well with the Diplock–Goddard–Dixon view.

Even the existence of an official ban on such morality-based verdicts does not necessarily favour the view that juries should declare what they believe rather than what they accept. Perhaps the standard procedure for banning those verdicts is to require the jury to swear to heed the evidence. Etymologically, after all, a juror *is* an oath-taker. Now suppose a juror does have to take a suitable oath, like the English one: 'I will faithfully try the defendant and give a true verdict according to the evidence.' Then what has to be kept in mind is that swearing an oath to perform a particular act commits one to believing, at the time the oath is taken, that it is within one's power to perform that act. For it follows from the existence of this commitment that what an English juror swears to do is to *accept* the consequences of the evidence. He cannot swear that his beliefs will be in accordance with the evidence because his beliefs are inherently involuntary and not within his power to create. In short, where jurors have to take an oath, the argument from the black-box character of their deliberations is overridden by the implications of their oath-taking.

Of course, though a juror cannot control his beliefs, he can in principle control certain other factors (such as his attention to witnesses' testimony or to the judge's admonitions) that may or may not cause beliefs about the issue to arise in him. Indeed by controlling those other factors he may even increase the probability that he has true beliefs about the defendant. But vowing to do what one can to produce the right beliefs in oneself is not the same as vowing actually to have the right state of mind. Compare how my promising to try to arrive by 5 p.m. is not the same as my promising, *tout court*, to arrive by 5 p.m. The latter commits me definitely to having the belief that I can arrive by 5 p.m., while the former does not. Correspondingly, the juror's oath is to give a true verdict according to the evidence, not just to try to give a true verdict according to the evidence.

Accordingly, if the interest of justice, or the public good, is promoted by a requirement that triers of fact be sworn, then the nature of the oath that would be appropriate for them entitles acceptance, rather than belief, to be considered the canonical mental state underlying their verdicts.

Perhaps someone will object that what a juror should swear to do is to pronounce in court (or in the jury-room) the verdict that he actually believes in his heart to be correct. The requirement of an oath, on this view, should be aimed at preventing any discrepancy between what the trier of fact believes and what he says. A juror's oath, like a witness's one, should promote candour and honesty.

But the objection will not stand. And my argument against the objection is not that certain existing oaths, like the English one, are not of the kind said by the objector to be needed. It is rather that oaths of the latter kind do not cover all that is needed. What good is it for a juror to tell the court exactly what he believes if his belief is the result of bias, prejudice, inattention, or fallacy? How can justice be done unless the conclusion accepted by the juror be adequately defensible? Whatever is accepted by him should be accepted for the reasons supplied by the data before the court. So the oath taken by a juror must be directed towards preserving the conformity not only of what he says to what he thinks but also of what he thinks to what are the data before the court. And for the latter purpose—just as well as for the former—it must be his voluntary acts of reasoned acceptance that count, not his involuntary states of induced belief.

Another important factor that has to be taken into account here is the extent to which the legal system regulates proof. Any such regulation tends to attract attention to the possibility of a divergence between belief and acceptance as the mental foundation for a juror's verdict. This is because, when the rule is stated or applied by a presiding judge, it tends to focus a juror's attention on what he is, or is not, entitled to accept in virtue of it—irrespective of what he believes. For example, where a proof depends at any point on a presumption, such as a presumption of legitimacy or of guilty knowledge, a lay trier of fact may be able to accommodate the presumed truth as a reason for accepting the proposed conclusion but be quite incapable of coming to believe that conclusion. Again, where the legal system requires corroboration for a certain type of testimony, such as the testimony of young children, a lay trier of fact may be inclined to believe the conclusions that flow from some piece of uncorroborated testimony but nevertheless be willing not to accept those conclusions as a basis for his verdict. This would be even more likely to happen where the relevant legal rule seemed rather a technical or artificial one, as with the old English rule that testimony requiring corroboration cannot corroborate testimony requiring corroboration. Similarly, if in the same trial some piece of evidence is admissible on one issue but not on another, it may be relatively easy for a jury to bear this in mind in relation to the conclusions that they accept, even though their beliefs are inevitably influenced by it on both issues. Indeed it is plausible to suppose that exclusionary rules, which help to determine acceptance-worthiness, have often entered the law of evidence in a particular legal system just because of the dangers that would exist if verdicts by lay tribunals were to be based on instinctive belief rather than considered acceptance in cases where the tribunal has unfortunately heard some potentially misleading evidence which it ought to disregard.

It follows that, if a legal system tends to have fairly extensive rules of evidence, this does not sit easily with the view that its verdicts should be regarded as expressing belief rather than acceptance. Correspondingly, where the nature of the judicial process is such as to generate a need for rules of evidence, one would expect triers of fact to declare what they accept rather than what they believe. So, if an adversarial—or predominantly adversarial—system, in regulating contests between proof and refutation, tends to require more rules of evidence than an inquisitorial one, it may also have a stronger tendency to subordinate belief to acceptance.

But it does not follow that an inquisitorial—or predominantly inquisitorial—system may not also work towards acceptance rather than belief. Such a system commonly, though not universally, operates without a separate jury or expert assessors, and with a single judge as both trier of fact and interpreter of law. And it is conceivable that the system might allow or require the judge not to weigh up the available facts or to try to derive a reasoned conclusion. His duty might be to consult his convictions after he has ingested all the relevant data. He would then be treating his subconscious mind as a kind of black box that takes evidence and legal knowledge as input and delivers verdicts as output. But an inquisitorial system does not have to operate like this. It could certainly expect to inspire greater public confidence in the correctness of its verdicts if these had to be supported by reasoning and the reasoning also had to be published. Where the trier of fact does not have to argue out the issues with colleagues, he ought at least to argue them out openly with himself, to guard against the obvious risks of bias, prejudice, over-confidence, or accidental paralogism. Rules about such reasoning could then, in effect, perform the same function in an inquisitorial system as is performed by rules about the presentation of evidence in an adversarial system.

Of course, it is in principle always possible for a solitary trier of fact to consult his private conviction first and construct his publicly announced justification afterwards, so as to present the appearance of having weighed up the arguments before coming to a conclusion. And this procedure, where it exists, may still be construed in terms of the domination of acceptance over belief, since it may be taken to reflect a determination on the judge's part to accept the conclusion that he believes instinctively to be correct rather than the conclusion at which he might arrive through conscious reasoning. But acceptance is not now playing so crucial a role, because it rides in only on the back of belief.

In sum, then, legal process does best to aim at verdicts that embody appropriately reasoned acceptance. In this it resembles scientific enquiry which, as we saw (§16), does best to aim at the acceptance of explanatory and predictive theories. In both cases the nature of the knowledge pursued requires adoption of an active rather than a passive attitude towards resolution of the issues. And, just as in scientific enquiry surrender to belief may harm the progress of science by blocking reconsideration of issues that need to be reconsidered, so too in trials of fact surrender to belief may obstruct the pursuit of justice by making it easier for illegitimate considerations to influence verdicts. If justice is to be done, the canonical purpose of advocacy ought to be to provide proofs or refutations that a rational trier of fact would accept. The canonical purpose ought not to be to engineer a desired state for the trier's credal feelings about the issue, even though this may in practice result.

Perhaps it will be objected that at least two standards of proof are commonly found in contemporary courts—a higher one for criminal cases and a lower one for civil cases. So we need, it will be said, to relate verdicts to a state of mind that comes in degrees. And belief does this while acceptance does not. You can believe strongly, or weakly, that *p*, but you either adopt the policy of premissing that *p* or you do not. Indeed, if degrees of belief are expressable as probabilities, the basing of verdicts on beliefs conveniently enables us to spell out the difference between different standards of proof in probabilistic terms: one standard requires the establishment of a probability of at least *x* per cent, another of at least *y* per cent. That is perhaps why those who analyse standards of juridical proof as thresholds of mathematical probability are often inclined to favour subjectivist, Ramsey-type analyses of probability.[43]

However, as already shown (§19), we cannot in fact treat subjective probabilities as degrees of belief. Instead, when it is necessary to specify gradations of proof, we can speak of the lowest odds that a trier of fact accepts as appropriate. Or, if it seems inappropriate to imagine how a jury would bet on the truth of a particular verdict when there is no way to settle the outcome of the bet, and if in any case a juror ought not to be thinking in terms of how he could expect to trade on his knowledge of the data about the case, then, more objectively, we can speak of the relative frequencies or causal propensities that he accepts as existing. Or, alternatively, we can speak of the superiority or conclusiveness of the reasons for accepting a particular verdict. So, whatever be the conception of probability in terms of which different standards of proof should be formulated,[44] it figures quite satisfactorily within a framework of acceptance.

Belief does, nevertheless, have one important role within the structure of courtroom thinking. In the standard type of case, belief is the attitude appropriate towards the data. To give testimony that *p* is normally to imply that one believes that *p* (see §14 above). And also the trier of fact must believe whatever propositions he takes as ultimate premisses—such as propositions about what the witnesses have said or about how they behave under cross-examination or about the familiar patterns of everyday life on which triers of fact rely in their reasonings. For it would be absurdly arbitrary if, by an act of unreasoned acceptance, a trier of fact could determine his ultimate premisses at will. Here again legal process is like scientific enquiry, where those who produce the original reports of experimental or observational data are assumed to believe their truth. But just as an expert witness, as distinct from an eyewitness, reports what he and his colleagues would *accept* within their relevant field of expertise, so too a scientific textbook may report data that the author of the textbook has not himself observed but nevertheless accepts as genuine.

[43] For example, D. Kaye, 'The Laws of Probability and the Law of the Land', *University of Chicago Law Review*, 47 (1979), pp. 34–56.
[44] This issue is discussed at length in Cohen, *The Probable and the Provable*.

§21. DO INTENTIONS IMPLY BELIEFS?

There is a well-known philosophical controversy about the relationship between a person's intention to do act *A* and his cognitive attitude towards the doing of that act.

On the one side Hampshire and Hart have argued that 'I have decided to do this' entails 'I am certain that I will do this, unless I am in some way prevented.'[45] So an agent's intention today to go to London tomorrow, they say, entails his not only believing but actually knowing today that he will go to London tomorrow unless he changes his mind or is prevented. And his knowledge is not based on any kind of induction from evidence. This kind of knowledge about the future is therefore to be distinguished from ordinary, inductive knowledge, whereby a person's actions may be predicted from the available evidence even when he has made no relevant decisions and formed no relevant intentions.[46]

On the other side Davidson has argued that such a thesis confuses what is conceptually entailed by a statement of intention with what is implied by making it. The person who under appropriate conditions sincerely avows, 'I intend to do act *A*', must believe that he will, unless prevented, do act *A*. Otherwise his utterance would be misleading, since it certainly constitutes evidence that, other things being equal, he will do act *A*. He ought not to provide such evidence for others to use, if he does not himself believe that he will do act *A*. But it is the avowal, not the intention, that implies the belief here.[47]

Of course this argument does not go far enough, as Davidson recognizes since it applies only to cases in which the intender avows his intention, whereas there seems to be some intuitive support for the view that even silent intentions carry with them some cognitive implications. So what is needed, on Davidson's side of the argument, is to counter such intuitions by an obviously conflicting example. Consider, accordingly, a person who is writing heavily on a sheet of paper, intending to produce ten legible carbon

---

[45] S. Hampshire and H. L. A. Hart, 'Decision, Intention and Certainty', *Mind*, 67 (1958), p. 2.

[46] Ibid. pp. 2–5.

[47] D. Davidson, *Essays on Actions and Events* (Oxford: Clarendon Press, 1982), p. 91.

copies. He may not know or believe that he is succeeding. But, according to Davidson, if he is producing ten legible copies, he is certainly doing what he intends to do.[48] And it has also been pointed out[49] that in any case the cognition allegedly implicit in intentions is strikingly devoid of analogy with what we ordinarily call 'belief' if it is in principle not open to confirmation or disconfirmation by relevant evidence.

In order to reconcile these conflicting intuitions and arguments it is tempting to claim that they arise from an underlying ambiguity. Perhaps one needs to acknowledge, as Harman has done,[50] some more elementary act or attitude of 'willing' that is encapsulated within every intention but can also occur on its own. Thus Harman supposes that a person intends to do act *A* if and only if he wills to do it and also believes that his present will to do it will result, *ceteris paribus*, in his doing it. It is then possible to treat the widely present association of the willing with the believing in such cases as a merely contingent psychological constraint, while the relationship between the intending and the believing is a conceptually necessary one. In this way, it seems, justice can be done to both sides of the argument. The person who intends to produce ten legible copies must believe that, unless prevented, he will do so, but the person who wills to produce them need not believe this. Hence arises the intuition that intentions involve a special, noninductive form of knowledge about the future. But the person who wills to produce ten legible copies is just under psychological pressure to believe that they will be produced. Hence—by a confusion of will with intention—arises the intuition that intentions to do act *A* do not entail beliefs that, unless prevented, act *A* will be done.

Unfortunately, however, Harman's resolution of the controversy, like the controversy itself, fails to allow for the fact that the concept of a belief is the concept of an involuntary disposition. Because of that fact no state of mind that conceptually implies a belief can itself be under a person's direct control. More specifically, an

[48] Ibid. p. 92.

[49] H. P. Grice, *Intention and Uncertainty* (London: Oxford University Press, 1971), pp. 7–8.

[50] G. Harman, 'Willing and Intending', in R. E. Grandy and R. Warner (eds.), *Philosophical Grounds of Rationality: Intentions, Categories, Ends* (Oxford: Clarendon Press, 1986), pp. 363–80.

intention to do act *A* cannot entail belief that, unless prevented, act *A* will occur, since the formation of an intention is in principle under the intender's own direct control while the formation of a belief is in principle not under the believer's direct control. That is why you are responsible for your intentions but not for your beliefs (see §§4 and 7 above).

But it does not follow that intentions have no cognitive implications. There is still room to insist on the existence of a connection between a person's intention to do act *A* and his cognitive attitude towards the proposition that, unless prevented, he will do act *A*. It is just that the relevant cognitive attitude should be conceived to be that of acceptance, not belief. And, if he announces his attitude, the announcement is an assertion (§13), not a prediction. The point is that anyone who seriously intends to do act *A* thereby commits himself, in his own mind, to taking it as a premiss that, unless prevented, he will do act *A*. If he doesn't adopt the policy of taking this as a premiss, he can't seriously intend to do it. For example, it would be absurd to say: 'George currently intends to go to London tomorrow but is currently not basing his plans on the premiss that, if he is not prevented, he will go to London tomorrow.' One wants to ask: 'How could he not be describable as ready to base his plans or other reasoning on his going to London tomorrow if that is what he intends to do?' Doesn't his forming the intention to do act *A* necessarily include adopting the policy of taking it that, unless prevented, this is what he will do? But a failure to distinguish adequately between belief and acceptance is bound to generate conflicting intuitions about the matter.

Accordingly, the knowledge or certainty that an intender has about his own future action should be said to have acceptance, not belief, at its core. Belief may be present in addition but its presence is not conceptually necessitated—any more than, as we have seen (in §17), it is necessitated in the case of scientific knowledge. It is conceivable that you may form an intention to make ten carbon copies of what you are writing but lack the disposition to feel that, unless prevented, you will succeed in doing this. No element of commitment connects an intention conceptually with the corresponding belief, in the way that it connects an intention with the corresponding acceptance. If you genuinely intend to make ten copies, as you press on the paper, then you are rationally committed to including the fulfilment of that intention among the premisses for your reasoning on other issues. Only thus does it constitute a coherent part of your current plans. But, of course, a determined and self-confident individual will be much more inclined than a consciously weak-willed one also to have beliefs corresponding to his intentions.

Moreover, it is now apparent how the cognitive attitude that goes along with intentions can afford to dispense with confirmation or disconfirmation by available evidence and yet remain a rational mental attitude. For, as remarked earlier (pp. 12 and 20), acceptance can be supported by ethical or prudential reasons as well as, or instead of, by evidential ones. And obviously that kind of support is available for acceptances implicit in intentions. The very same facts that are reasons for a person's intending to do act *A* must also be reasons for anything that is conceptually implicit in this intending. If the reason why George intends to go to London tomorrow is to buy a new hat, then that must ultimately also be a reason why he accepts that, unless prevented, he will indeed go to London.

It is a different matter, however, if we consider not merely the nature of this cognitive mental attitude that goes along with intention but also the status of that attitude. We then need to ask, how can such an acceptance, even when thought correct, be said to constitute knowledge? Remember that a person's ethical or prudential reasons for intending to do act *A*, and for thus implicitly accepting that he will do *A*, are not reasons of the type that can justify this acceptance in the way that would be requisite for it to constitute an item of knowledge. As we have already noted (pp. 102–3), he needs evidential or methodological reasons for this purpose, not ethical or prudential ones. But it is not difficult to see what such reasons must be. They must be inductive reasons for accepting that he will not change his mind. A person who, when he intends to do act *A*, also *knows* that he will do act *A* (unless prevented by factors over which he has no control) is a person who has good reasons to be confident of his own determination. Perhaps, for example, he remembers having resisted the temptation to change his mind on similar, past occasions. A person who has no such reason can hardly be said to *know* that he will, in the event, actually do *A*, despite the fact that he now intends to do so.

Of course, in a sense—the sense in which knowledge implies acceptance rather than belief—a person can always be said to know even more than he intends. This is because acceptance, as we have seen (§5), is subjectively closed under deducibility, whereas intention, like belief, is not. A person may be described *de dicto* as intending to give a million pounds to charity without having the intention to give 10^6 pounds to charity, even though he knows that his giving 10^6 pounds is deducible from his giving a million pounds. But if he does intend to give a million pounds to charity, and is confident of his determination to do this, and knows that his giving 10^6 pounds is deducible from his giving a million, then he certainly knows that, unless prevented, he will be giving 10^6 pounds to charity.

§22. WHEN IS BELIEF A REASON FOR ACCEPTANCE?

It has already emerged (§3) that there are important ways in which a person's states of belief can justify his acts of acceptance. In ordinary cases of perception and memory, a person's possession of a belief that p is a presumptive reason for him to accept that p. If on looking out of the window you form the belief that it is raining, you should normally accept that it is, and if on consulting your memory you form the belief that you left your keys in the kitchen you should normally accept that you did. And the situation in regard to scientific data (pp. 92–3) is just a special case of this. When a scientific investigator asserts that p, in the course of reporting his experimental data, he can normally cite his possession of the relevant beliefs as sufficient support for anyone's accepting that p. Indeed, if he cannot honestly do this, he ought not to have published his report.

But are there any other categories of what we may conveniently call 'presumptively acceptable beliefs', besides those due to the processes of sensation or memory? And, if not, why not?

Consider, for example, a mistaken belief about how Nature works, such as the old belief that inhalation of swampy air is the cause of malarial fever. Because such mistaken beliefs are quite common, and sometimes exist for centuries, it is scarcely plausible to regard them as mere freaks or anomalies like the momentary beliefs that are due to visual illusions. They compel us rather to admit that, since beliefs about how Nature works can so often be deeply mistaken, they are not to be regarded as presumptively acceptable beliefs. So what is the crucial difference between the kind of mechanism that generates presumptively acceptable beliefs and the kind that generates beliefs which are not presumptively acceptable? This question has to be answered if we are to gain a sufficiently thorough understanding of the relationship between belief and acceptance. And the answer seems to be that, wherever there is standardly some opportunity for the intrusion of a voluntary element into the mechanism, the kind of belief generated is not presumptively acceptable, because a mistake may be made in the discharge of this voluntary element. For example, in the case of a belief about how Nature works, we do not have to rely passively on the evidence that comes our way but we can, and indeed should, seek actively to vary the circumstances in which we test our hypotheses. If we do not do this, we may let ourselves be misled by the accidental presence—in our passive experience—of some factor that is not causally relevant, as by the presence of swampy air in the case of the old belief about malaria. On the other hand, there is ordinarily no opportunity for the intrusion of a voluntary element into the processes by which we acquire perceptual beliefs or memories. Of course, by wearing glasses, hearing-aids, etc. you can affect the perceptual sensations you have. But under normal circumstances you can't affect the impact of your sensations—such as they are—on your belief-system. Once the sensations have occurred, the corresponding beliefs ensue.

How far is this conceptual structure echoed where the issues involved are normative rather than factual, as when, for example, a person's logical insight or moral conscience is construed—albeit metaphorically—as being an engine of intuitive belief? Sidgwick certainly held that a general moral principle can derive support directly from the existence of intuitive belief in its correctness.[51] And such a doctrine is tenable if one supposes, like Joseph Butler,[52] that God has provided each of us with a conscience that resolves correctly any moral quandary submitted to its arbitration. On that supposition there is no room for the agent to argue legitimately against the dictates of this Divine mechanism. But, if appeals to intuition lack such a theistic foundation, they are in principle open to being countered by voluntary appeals to other considerations,

---

[51] H. Sidgwick, *The Methods of Ethics*, 7th edn. (London: Macmillan, 1907), pp. 96–103.

[52] J. Butler, *The Works of Joseph Butler, DCL*, ed. W. E. Gladstone (Oxford: Clarendon Press, 1896), vol. ii, sermons II and III.

whether these be Kantian, utilitarian, or whatever. In short, without the theistic foundation normative beliefs or intuitions are not presumptively acceptable (although they may well reinforce one another in ways that support accepting their systematization[53]).

Another type of situation where the existence of a person's belief that *p* cannot provide any reason at all for his accepting that *p* is where he both believes that *p* and believes that not-*p*. We saw earlier (in §6) that, where the beliefs are not strong ones, a person is indecisive rather than irrational if he has contradictory beliefs. This holds good not only in relation to factual beliefs but also in relation to normative ones. Just as you can half-believe that you heard a sound at the door and half-believe that you did not, so too you can half-believe that you ought to send a donation to the animal liberation movement and half-believe that you ought not. But it would be irrational, as we saw (in §6), to accept that *p* while also accepting that not-*p*. So it would produce irrational conclusions if we allowed the existence of a belief to support the corresponding acceptance in cases in which two of the propositions believed are mutually contradictory. Instead, other supporting arguments need to be brought in (as Hare makes clear in his discussion of the transition from intuitive to critical moral thinking[54]), and this point also has an important application where the propositions are about philosophical issues: philosophers who claim that we cannot avoid having inconsistent *beliefs* about reality should feel an obligation to present a consistent account of reality for our *acceptance*. Thus Nagel succeeds in showing[55] how belief in the subjective nature of reality may conflict in someone's mind with belief in its objective nature: I both am and am not the hub of the Universe. But any conclusion he suggests that we ought to be content to accept both conceptions of reality is an irrational one. At best Nagel can be described as stating a central philosophical paradox without resolving it, at worst as offering an irrational syncretism for its resolution.

[53] These issues are discussed more fully in Cohen, *The Dialogue of Reason*, 49–147.

[54] See R. M. Hare, *Moral Thinking: Its Levels, Method and Point* (Oxford: Clarendon Press, 1981), pp. 25–43.

[55] T. Nagel, *The View from Nowhere* (Oxford: Clarendon Press, 1986).

V

Self-Deceit and the Socratic Paradox

We want to be able to say (§23) that people sometimes deliberately deceive themselves. Yet the accusation of self-deceit seems conceptually paradoxical. Various familiar proposals for the resolution of the paradox are unsatisfactory (§24). What we have to suppose instead (§25) is that in self-deceit the suppressed thought is characteristically a belief that, say, not-*p*, while what the person deceives himself into doing—by fiddling with the evidential books—is to accept that *p*. Similarly (§26), various familiar proposals for resolving the Socratic paradox about moral self-control are unsatisfactory. And what we have to show instead (§27) is how an agent's belief that he is not to do a particular act may be consistent with accepting that he is to do it. Nor will it do (§28)—either in the paradox of self-deceit or in the Socratic paradox—to say that what is suppressed is an act of acceptance and what takes its place is a belief.

§23. THE PARADOX OF SELF-DECEPTION

The accusation that a person is deceiving himself slips easily off the tongue in certain circumstances. Paul apparently thinks, against the obvious balance of his evidence, that his beloved will agree to marry him, because that is what he would like to happen. George apparently thinks, against the obvious balance of his evidence, that he is an interesting conversationalist, because that is what he would like to be. John apparently thinks, against the obvious balance of his evidence, that his motive for reading a low-brow newspaper is not prurience but academic curiosity, because that is what he would like his motive to be. In situations of this type, people often nowadays affirm that a person is deceiving himself. And novelists like Henry James or Marcel Proust have constructed rich and subtle stories about more complex cases of self-deception, exploring the variety of its motivations, the intricacies of its consequences, the difficulties that attempts to dispel it encounter, or the poignant outcomes of its disappearance. At the same time psychoanalysts often diagnose self-deception in their patients, and political theorists may claim that large sections of the population deceive themselves about their real motives or circumstances. Though ancient, medieval, or early modern European literature, or the early records of non-European civilizations, do not reveal much clear interest in self-deception of this kind in everyday secular life, the idea has certainly had a long history in theology[1] and has become a commonplace of modern culture.

Even in the ancient world, of course, people were often described as 'deceiving themselves'. But this description seems then to have operated mainly as a hyperbole for 'being mistaken through their own fault'.[2] It seems not to have normally implied some kind of intellectual dishonesty, such as that whereby the desire that p might unconsciously motivate a person to suppress his memory of evidence favouring the proposition that not-p. Indeed, no such implication could become normal until the possibility of unconscious states and processes in the mind was widely admitted. And that admission seems to have widened only gradually in western Europe from the sixteenth century onwards. It took Shakespeare, Spinoza, Leibniz, and many others to contribute to the widening.[3]

However, the newer conception of self-deception has not altogether driven out the older one. We can still speak also of unintentional self-deception, where nothing deceitful occurs because no desire to deceive is either consciously or unconsciously operative. Consider an analogous two-party case first. As the driver of a car rather irresponsibly waves to a friend out of his window, he may unintentionally, and without desiring it, deceive you into thinking that he is signalling a change of direction. One-party cases work correspondingly. For example, if—because of an interruption immediately after arranging it—I quite accidentally, though rather carelessly, fail to write down in my diary an appointment for next Tuesday, I may unintentionally, and without desiring it, deceive

---

[1] On Augustine's use of the idea see B. C. van Fraassen, 'The Peculiar Effects of Love and Desire', in B. M. McLaughlin and A. O. Rorty (eds.), *Perspectives on Self-Deception* (Berkeley: University of California Press, 1988), pp. 123–56. See also Joseph Butler's sermon on self-deceit, in W. E. Gladstone (ed.), *The Works of Joseph Butler, DCL* (Oxford: Clarendon Press, 1896), ii. 168–84.

[2] For example, Plato, *Cratylus*, 428D3–4, and Cicero, *Philippics*, xii. 8, 21.

[3] For references see L. L. Whyte, *The Unconscious Before Freud* (London: Tavistock Publications, 1962), pp. 59–176.

myself thereby into thinking later that I have a free and uncommitted afternoon that day. There is no self-deceit here, but only self-deception, if no desire to deceive has unconsciously motivated me. It seems reasonable therefore to ask: how is self-deceit possible? Consider first what ordinary two-party deceit involves. If A is said intentionally to deceive another person, B, into thinking that p, then A himself is implied to think—quite unquestioningly—that not-p, and therefore not to think that p. (It wouldn't be sufficient for him merely to lack the thought that p or just to have a slight inclination to think that not-p: in such cases he might be described as being over-eager to get B to think that p, but this would hardly amount to deceit.) Moreover, not only must A himself think that not-p and not have the thought that p, he must also want and intend to bring it about that B thinks that p. So B's state is changed by A's action from one in which B himself does not have the thought that p to one in which he does, while at least for the moment A's thought that not-p remains unchanged.

Now suppose that A and B are one and the same person, so that the deceit may be called 'self-deceit'. It must now apparently be the case both that A thinks that p and that A lacks the thought that p. And in addition it must be the case both that A's thought on the issue—the issue whether or not it is true that p—is changed, as he wants and intends it to be, and also that A's thought on the issue is unchanged. The derivation of these formal contradictions is apparently undeniable. No such paradox arises in relation to a person's accidental or unintentional self-deception, because there, at the time at which he thinks the mistaken thought, he is not supposed also to think the unmistaken one. But it looks as though self-deceit must be impossible, because description of it is self-contradictory. Apparently we can never be entitled to describe anyone as having intentionally, or at least non-accidentally, deceived himself. And yet it seems intuitively natural and intelligible to describe someone thus. So, whatever other paradoxes there may be about self-deception, we certainly have here a philosophical paradox of the classical kind, like Zeno's or Russell's antinomy, where some apparently natural and intelligible way of speaking—about motion, say, or about sets or about thoughts—is nevertheless demonstrated to generate a contradiction.

In short, the fact of self-deceit seems familiar and scarcely controversial, but we need a coherent pattern of description for it.

It is perhaps just worth noting, however, that not all conceivable cases of self-deceit are exposed to this paradox. For example, one can imagine an amnesic drug that a person takes when he realizes that he is about to undergo an unpleasant or embarrassing experience. The purpose of taking the drug might be to avoid having any unpleasant or embarrassing memories afterwards—even memories of taking the drug itself. So by taking the drug at one time a person intentionally deceives himself into thinking at the later time that he did not take the drug at the earlier time. Yet there is obviously no time at which he both thinks and does not think the same thought, and it is equally obvious that his relevant thought has changed and is not unchanged. I shall disregard such cases here, since they seem conceptually unparadoxical (whether or not they are neurologically possible).

§24. SOME PROPOSED RESOLUTIONS OF THE PARADOX
OF SELF-DECEPTION

Various inadequate resolutions of the paradox have been put forward by philosophers. It will be convenient to discuss three different kinds of these.

According to one account,[4] the concept of self-deception should be interpreted as a species of self-command. Self-deception is then said to resemble commanding a person who obeys the command though strongly disinclined to do so, because this disinclination is said to resemble the situation in which the self-deceived thinker has the weight of the evidence against him. No contradiction is then involved because no contrary command is also supposed, only a disinclination to obey the one command.

But the trouble is that any such comparison emasculates the concept of self-deceit. No bad faith, no element of intellectual dishonesty need be present in the mind of someone who tells himself to do something that he is strongly disinclined to do because of its unwelcome consequences. Indeed, such a person is presumably fully conscious of the unwelcome consequences that disincline him to obey the command. So, since no relevant data are

---

[4] J. V. Canfield and D. F. Gustafson, 'Self-Deception', *Analysis*, 23 (1962), pp. 32–6.

being kept out of sight or out of mind, there is no room for any accusation of trickery. And this is very different from what we may take to be the typical case of self-deceit—where a person definitely turns his attention away from the evidence or inferences that run counter to his cherished delusion.

Perhaps we should therefore consider another account,[5] which does pay more attention to the treatment of the evidence. According to this account, what characterizes the self-deceiver is that his thoughts about certain issues seem to conflict with what an objective judge would infer from the evidential data, despite the fact that, as he indicates, he is clearly aware in his own mind of the existence and significance of these data. For example, we can imagine a political leader who is under no illusion that the evidence objectively favours the success of the military enterprise that he plans, but nevertheless persists in attempting it through some deep-seated faith in his own destiny.

But here the issue is trivialized. We are offered little more than a conscious conflict between the results of applying different prima facie criteria for the correctness of an answer to a given question, with an effective preference—when everything is taken into consideration—for the more subjectively supported opinion. And this again does less than justice to the accusation of intellectual dishonesty that is implicit in the charge of self-deceit. The self-deceiver does not allow himself to have fully in mind the existence and significance of the data that run counter to his preferred opinion. That is how he deceives himself: he conceals a vital part of the evidence from his own scrutiny and proper appraisal. Of course, the term 'self-deception' is no doubt often used loosely so as to cover cases like that of the political leader. But those are not the usages that seem to generate formal contradictions. The paradox arises because there is a sense of the term in which we feel that it is a tight and accurate description of certain human situations— and yet *apparently* a self-contradictory description of them.

According to a third account, therefore, we have to suppose that two different cognitive systems are at work in the mind of the self-deceiver, with the one system deliberately concealing or misinterpreting relevant facts so as to deceive the other system into holding

[5] T. Penelhum, 'Pleasure and Falsity', *American Philosophical Quarterly*, 1 (1964), pp. 87–91.

the preferred but erroneous opinion. This account at last seems to pay due attention to the element of bad faith that is implicit in an act of self-deceit. But the analysis raises a further question. How can two such systems coexist within the mind of a single person?

A Freudian version[6] of the analysis would answer that question by supposing the existence of a 'censor' which separates the conscious 'ego' from the contents of his unconscious 'id'. It is thus the 'censor' that keeps the unwanted opinion buried in the unconscious and allows the conscious 'ego'—the main system of thoughts and desires that runs a person's daily life—to operate independently of that opinion. Paul's 'ego' is able to think quite rationally that his beloved returns his affection because his 'censor' has suppressed any memory or appreciation of the contrary evidence.

The Freudian resolution of the paradox is open to the obvious objection, as Sartre saw,[7] that the so-called 'censor' is nothing but an internal manikin that both knows the true facts and also buries them. So the manikin is just another self-deceiver and the paradox breaks out again. Admittedly this objection might be met by supposing that only the 'censor' is aware of the true fact and only the 'ego' is in error. The 'censor' is not then a self-deceiver and its characterization creates no paradox. And philosophers have suggested various other ingenious methods of dividing the relevant mental activity between two systems in such a way that, though neither system separately is guilty of self-deceit, the symbiotic combination of the two systems contrives to reconstitute the self-deceit of a unitary mind.[8] The relevant mental activity that is to be divided up may contain, in a typical case, at least the following ten elements along with their causal interconnections: the awareness of facts which are evidence that not-p, the awareness of norms which are norms for interpreting what such facts indicate, the thought that on the evidence it is rational to think that not-p, the

---

[6] For example, S. Freud, *The Interpretation of Dreams*, in J. Strachey (ed.), *The Complete Psychological Works of Sigmund Freud* (London: Hogarth Press, 1953), iv. 234–6.

[7] J.-P. Sartre, *Being and Nothingness*, trans. H. E. Barnes (London: Methuen, 1957), pp. 50–3.

[8] For example, D. Davidson, 'Paradoxes of Irrationality', in R. Wollheim and J. Hopkins (eds.), *Philosophical Essays on Freud* (Cambridge: Cambridge University Press, 1982), pp. 289–305; and D. F. Pears, *Motivated Irrationality* (Oxford: Clarendon Press, 1984), pp. 67–106. See also P. L. Gardiner, 'Error, Faith and Self-Deception', *Proceedings of the Aristotelian Society*, 70 (1970), pp. 221–43.

thought that not-p, a desire for it to be true that p, a suppression or prevention of awareness of the relevant evidence or of thought about its interpretation, a suppression or prevention of the thought that not-p, a shift of attention towards supposed reasons for thinking that p, the thought that on the evidence it is rational to think that p, and—finally—the thought that p. So there is plenty of room for variety of division within the two-systems analysis. All that is needed is not to allocate mutually inconsistent elements, such as the thought that not-p and the thought that p, to the same system.

But any version of the two-systems analysis is open, whatever else its flaws, to the objection that it attempts to answer the question 'How is self-deceit possible?' by an *ignoratio elenchi*. The analysis assumes the existence of two manikins in the self-deceiver's mind, each of whom is equipped with some subset or other of the familiar list of cognitions and motivations. Their mode of operation is therefore characterized by an ascription of predicates to which we are to attach the usual meanings that they have when predicated of real, whole, full-scale people. And we understand how the manikins operate only because we understand those meanings in everyday life. Indeed we are told quite clearly even by Pears—the most subtle advocate of a two-systems analysis—that 'the model for the two systems is two people'.[9] Yet in this way the analysis inevitably fails to get to the core of the problem. The core question to be answered is how it is possible for a single individual to deceive himself. And the two-systems analysis doesn't answer this question. It gives us an answer instead to the question 'What is the most jejune distribution of the relevant cognitions and motivations that will make it possible for one person to deceive another? That is, what are the minimal states of mind that must be attributed to the deceiver, and what are the minimal states of mind that must then be attributed to the deceived?' What we wanted to know was how such an array of mutually interacting states of mind can co-occur in a single person, and what we are told instead is how they can be divided up between two people.

One cannot help wondering why anyone could ever have supposed that the philosophical paradox can be resolved in this way. Perhaps it was because at times the underlying question, 'How is

[9] *Motivated Irrationality*, p. 97.

self-deceit possible?', was thought of as posing a causal, psychological problem rather than a conceptual, analytical one. Compare contexts in which the question 'How is induction possible?' may be taken to pose a psychological problem about the human ability to generalize from given individual instances rather than an epistemological problem about our logical entitlement to generalize from such instances.

There is indeed a causal, psychological problem about self-deceit. But resolution of the philosophical problem is a prior necessity. Only when the phenomenon of self-deceit has been clearly and coherently characterized can we profitably search for the underlying mechanisms that explain it. We need to know what it is that has to be explained before we can be in a position to evaluate the success of a proposed explanation. That is why it is better not to suppose that a vocabulary like that of psychoanalytic theory, which is developed for the purpose of constructing deep psychological explanations, is appropriate also for the task of coherently describing important kinds of irrationality that may call for explanation.[10]

Contemporary philosophers' talk about 'two systems' can be confusing in this respect, because it carries just a hint of an underlying explanation's being available in computational terms—an explanation by reference to interacting modularities or homunculi that might rival the Freudian mythology about an 'ego', an 'id', and a 'censor'. Indeed, some contemporary empirical psychologists have proposed a two-systems postulate in order to explain certain experimental data about dissonance and cognitive attribution.[11] And Stich, as we have seen (§15), argues in favour of such a postulate as against the principle of unified cognition that he mistakenly attributes to folk psychology. More specifically, it may well be (pp. 57–8) that the fact that people can believe as well as accept is best explained by the coexistence of connectionist and digital systems of computation within the human brain. But when we examine closely what philosophers of self-deception (like Pears)

[10] *Pace*, for example, D. Davidson, 'Paradoxes of Irrationality', p. 304.
[11] For example, D. A. Norman, 'Reflections on Cognition and Parallel Distributed Processing', in D. E. Rumelhart and J. L. McClelland (eds.), *Parallel Distributed Processing: Explorations in the Microstructure of Cognition*, vol. ii: *Psychological and Biological Models* (Cambridge, Mass.: MIT Press, 1986), pp. 531–46.

offer as a characterization of their 'two systems', we cannot properly describe it as a psychological explanation, whether of the computational type or of any other kind. We do not in fact find any underlying architectures, algorithms, programs, program-sketches, or other productive mechanisms suggested. We find instead just a use of the usual, everyday, mentalistic vocabulary—'evidence', 'interpretation', 'thought', 'wish', etc.—which describes what is supposed to be going on without explaining how it can come about. Use of *that* vocabulary within a two-systems account makes the account at best relevant only to the conceptual, not the psychological, problem. But it is, as we have already seen, quite unsuited to the resolution of that problem, because it paints a picture of one person's deceiving another, not of a person's deceiving himself.

§25. SELF-DECEIT AS A CASE OF ACCEPTANCE DOMINATING BELIEF

Turn instead to the distinction between belief and acceptance. This distinction lends itself straightforwardly to the construction of a quite consistent description of what is going on in a case of self-deceit.

We have seen in previous chapters that, although there is a natural and mostly harmless tendency for the two to run together, there are cases in which belief and acceptance do not, or should not, coincide. Sometimes, for example, the proposition that is believed does not deserve acceptance, perhaps because the belief originates in a confused memory, a perceptual illusion, or a hallucination. Sometimes it is right to accept that p, perhaps as a matter of charity or of professional ethics or for some other pragmatic reason, even if you have no beliefs about the matter or believe the opposite. Sometimes, because of how other people react to the evidence, it may be quite reasonable for you to accept that p even though you have more than half a hunch that not-p. Sometimes, as in theoretical science, or historical research, or police detection, or military intelligence, it may be right to accept the hypothesis that p but undesirable to have any belief that p (§16). And other cases are connected with variations in the form of purposive explanation (§§7–12), with the implications of different types of indicative-sentence speech-acts (§§13–14), with a person's attribution of his own behaviour to specified causes (§15), with subjective probability (§19), with fact-finding in courts of law (§20), and so on.

The key to understanding the conceptual structure of self-deceit is to treat it as yet another species of the kind of case in which belief and acceptance fail to coincide. Specifically, the suppressed thought is characteristically a belief that not-*p*, while what the person deceives himself in doing is finding reasons to accept that *p* (or vice versa). It is thus possible for the same person at the same time to have opposed states of mind about the proposition that *p*. He believes but does not accept that not-*p*, say, while he accepts but does not believe that *p*. So there is no need to suppose two manikins interacting with one another. A single person is the subject of all the relevant mental predicates. Moreover, this account ensures that the rather complex state of self-deceit is attributable only to grown persons and not to infants, animals, or human organizations. Infants and animals cannot literally be said to deceive themselves about anything because they are capable only of belief, not of acceptance (as we saw in §9). And human organizations cannot literally be said to deceive themselves about anything[12] because they are capable only of acceptance, not of belief (as we saw in §10). Indeed, if human organizations are not even capable of belief, they are *a fortiori* incapable of suppressing their beliefs.

What, then, distinguishes self-deceit from other states of mind in which belief and acceptance fail to coincide?

One distinctive feature is obviously the fact that the self-deceiver, who consciously accepts that *p*, does not *consciously* believe that not-*p*. He has somehow put the belief that not-*p* out of mind. But how has he done this? Beliefs, as we saw (in §4), are involuntary. They cannot just be cast off at the will of the would-be self-deceiver. But in fact the self-deceiver does not lose his belief that not-*p* altogether. If he did, the process of self-deceit would have come to an end. What happens is that the belief is somehow suppressed, not eliminated. It remains, but not in consciousness. And that is possible because belief is a disposition—specifically, a

---

[12] *Pace* R. Scruton, 'Corporate Persons', *Proceedings of the Aristotelian Society*, Supp. vol. 63 (1989), p. 248.

disposition to feel it true that so-and-so—and dispositions can continue to exist while unactivated, just as a piece of rubber may still be flexible even though at the moment unbent. Hence, so far as a person can control the activation or non-activation of a belief-disposition, he can be said to be capable of keeping the belief intentionally or unintentionally out of his mind—i.e. out of his consciousness—while retaining the belief itself. And in practice we do very often control the activation or non-activation of our belief-dispositions even when we are in no way deceiving ourselves. For example, we may intentionally activate a belief that we have a committee-meeting at noon when we successfully search our memory for information about what we have to do at noon; and we unintentionally deactivate a belief that the cat is in the garden when we begin to wonder where on earth the dog can be. So there is nothing particularly mysterious about the fact that the self-deceiver manages to deactivate his belief that not-p. Occupied as he is, on relevant occasions, with his wish or desire that p, with his sustained consideration of the evidence that he takes to support his acceptance that p, and with his actually taking it as a premiss that p, he intentionally or unintentionally leaves himself no room to continue activating his belief that not-p on relevant occasions. Or perhaps he leaves himself no room even to begin activating it. Any occurrent manifestation of that belief gets crowded out.

Such a state of mind is not just ordinary wishful thinking. But we have to be careful about specifying where it differs from the latter. According to Davidson's view of the difference,[13] wishful thinking is always directed towards satisfying some desire, whereas in self-deception the thought that is generated may be an unwelcome one, as when a person who deceives himself into thinking that his beloved is unfaithful identifies evidence for his jealousy everywhere. This point of Davidson's, however, is not a strong one. Those who deceive themselves into states of mind that people normally try to avoid tend to be regarded, for that very reason, as being warped, 'neurotic', or maladjusted. They may be thought of as mental masochists who want to wallow in their own misery. An element of unconscious desire is so deeply embedded in the concept

---

[13] D. Davidson, 'Deception and Division', in E. Lepore and B. M. McLaughlin (eds.), *Actions and Events, Perspectives on the Philosophy of Donald Davidson* (Oxford: Blackwell, 1985), p. 144.

of self-deceit that, in cases where there is no other way to sustain the presence of that element, the self-deceiver may be viewed as a masochist rather than as a person who is distressed by his painful experience. So self-deception should not be taken to differ from wishful thinking in the way that Davidson supposes. Instead, what needs to be noted is that in ordinary wishful thinking we not only wish or desire that *p* and, as a result, come to think that *p*: we are all the more able—in ordinary wishful thinking—to come to think that *p* because we do not have a belief that not-*p*. And a consequence of our thus not having a belief that not-*p* is that no element of self-deceit can be attributed to us, since, just as an ordinary two-party deceiver is supposed to have a belief contrary to the thought that he is trying to inculcate, so too in the state of mind that I am claiming to be that of a self-deceiver, the old belief that not-*p* is supposed to persist, though dormant.

Even so, there must be more to self-deceit than I have so far described, because so far no element of intellectual dishonesty has revealed itself as being inherent in the situation. There is nothing necessarily dishonest, or inherently irrational, about driving the belief that not-*p* out of your consciousness when you wish that *p* and come to accept that *p*. If you have honestly come to accept that *p*, then, even if you cannot force yourself to discard altogether your involuntary belief that not-*p*, you are at least entitled to promote the deactivation of that belief. So what else is there to self-deceit than has so far been described?

The other distinctive feature of self-deceit that needs to be mentioned is the way in which the self-deceiver handles the evidence. And it is there that intellectual dishonesty or irrationality enters into the situation. No analysis that ignores this (as, for example, Bach's analysis does[14]) can be satisfactory. The genuine self-deceiver is the person who, because of his desire that *p*, either fails to accept some relevant premises in the case for not-*p* even though he believes them to be both relevant and true, or accepts some propositions as relevant premises in the case for *p* even though he does not believe them, or does both of these things. And those premises may be either pieces of relevant evidence or relevant norms for the interpretation of evidence. For example, the

[14] K. Bach, 'An Analysis of Self-Deception', *Philosophy and Phenomenological Research*, 41 (1981), pp. 351–70.

self-deceiving lover may put out of mind his recollection of seeing his beloved smile affectionately at another man. Or he may altogether suppress his disposition to feel that this event once occurred. Or perhaps he imagines that she once looked like that at him instead. Or perhaps he attaches too much weight—far more weight than he in general believes it right to attach to such evidence—to the fact that she once ended a letter to him with the words 'Love, Jane'. Thus the typical self-deceiver commits the epistemological crime of fiddling with the evidential books. That is his strategy of deceit, though he is unconscious of employing it as such. He may be said to deceive himself in this way just as surely as he may be said to deceive anyone else to whom he supplies false testimony or forged documents, or whom he deprives of some of the relevant evidence, or whom he misleads about how to interpret the evidence. Indeed, there can be no deceit at all—whether self-deceit or two-party deceit—unless there is some chicanery with the evidence currently available to the deceived. And when the self-deceiver has actually got good justification—which he is minded to ignore—for believing that not-p, he may be said not merely to believe, but actually to know, that not-p (see §17 above) when he accepts that p.

Notice, however, that what is supposed to trigger the self-deceit is typically a passive, involuntary desire that p. It can hardly be a conscious decision of any kind, or the adoption of a goal, or the deliberate formation of an intention. This desire is supposed to incline the self-deceiver towards unconsciously adopting a plan for systematically mishandling the evidence. So the self-deceiver is normally not held fully responsible for his own actions. And no doubt that is at least partly why, although we think of self-deceit as a species of intellectual dishonesty, we do not normally consider it to be a moral crime like the deception of others.

Davidson has argued instead that the motive for a person's deceitfully inducing the thought that p in himself is his belief that not-p. And in the strongest case, according to Davidson, the belief that not-p not only causes the thought that p but sustains it.[15] However, this is not a tenable position. Since the normal situation is for the belief that not-p *not* to be accompanied by the thought that p, what can count as a cause for the self-deceitful thought that

---

[15] Davidson, 'Deception and Division', p. 145.

p has to be something that differentiates the cases in which the belief that not-*p* comes to be accompanied by the thought that *p* from the cases in which it does not.

Of course, self-deceit comes in many different shapes and sizes, if we are to credit those who diagnose it. Sometimes the de-activation of the opposing belief is total, sometimes only partial. The person who just shrugs his shoulders at the evidence against accepting that *p* has obviously managed to suppress all conscious-ness of the power and implications of appropriate interpretative norms. If, instead, the self-deceiver spends a lot of time convincing himself that no such evidence undermines his acceptance that *p*, he has obviously not suppressed his beliefs about relevant norms so successfully. Perhaps he even has moments of self-doubt when the deactivated beliefs temporarily re-activate themselves. It is conceiv-able also that a person might trick himself into accepting that *p* when in fact it is true that *p* though he still believes—deep down—that not-*p*. But accusations of self-deceit, like accusations about the deception of others, are generally taken to imply that the accuser believes the deceiver to be concealing the truth from the deceived—not merely concealing what he (the deceiver) thinks to be the truth.

Self-deception varies widely in regard to topic. Sometimes a person is said to deceive himself about his own motives, emotions, or attitudes, sometimes about those of others, and sometimes about objects, events, or probabilities in the world around him. And another way in which one instance of self-deceit may differ from another is in respect of motivation. Sometimes what lies behind the desire that *p* is supposed to be hope, sometimes fear, sometimes pride, sometimes vanity, sometimes shame, sometimes jealousy, and so on. Apparently any reason for desiring that *p*, or any kind of reluctance or inability to live with a belief that not-*p*, can help to generate the self-deceiver's acceptance that *p*.

Perhaps someone will object that in certain cases of unintention-ally deceiving oneself about one's own motives, emotions, or attitudes, there is no room for fiddling with the evidential books because no evidence needs to be invoked. For instance, the person who deceives himself that he is in love with his friend just because he wants to be in love with her, is not to be understood as misinterpreting his own letters to her but as writing unconsciously insincere declarations of love in those letters. However, if we tried to persuade a person of this kind that he was deceiving himself, we should have to point to such facts as his awareness of his ability to concentrate for long periods on other matters, his awareness of his own reluctance to go out of his way to meet his friend, his awareness of his own failure to celebrate her return from abroad, and so on. And a persistent self-deceiver would then have to give us his deceptive gloss on each of these evidential facts—a gloss that would render the fact coherent with, or even supportive of, his accepted self-description.

Similarly, someone may actually enjoy making cruel jokes but deceive himself that he just indulges in witty repartee. It might be argued that in such a case there is no clash between what the self-deceiver believes and what he accepts, because what he keeps out of mind is his actual motive, not a belief about that motive. But one has to distinguish[16] here between being mistaken, through wishful thinking, about one's own motives or attitudes and actually deceiving oneself about them. If the cruel joker is not suppressing a true belief about his real motive, he is merely mistaken about that motive and not deceiving himself about it. Or at any rate he is not deceiving himself in a way that might generate the paradox of self-deceit (where someone seems both to think that p and not to think that p, and both to change his thought about whether p and not to change it).

Spotting self-deceit in yourself is a lot more difficult than spotting it in others, but your own self-deceit is intrinsically easier to eliminate once you have spotted it. For, once you accept that you have spotted self-deceit in yourself on some issue, it has presumably thereby ceased to exist in you on that issue. Since you now accept what you believe, you can no longer be suppressing that belief. But someone who has formed a habit of misinterpreting the evidence about a certain issue may well fail to appreciate the evidence—with which you supply him—that he needs re-educating in this respect. Indeed, although deceiving oneself, as an act of acceptance, always involves making a mistake voluntarily (and differs correspondingly from states of involuntary error such as those brought about by hypnosis, hallucination, etc.), that erroneous judgement

---

[16] As D. H. Sanford fails to do in 'Self-Deception as Rationalization', in B. M. McLaughlin and A. O. Rorty (eds.), *Perspectives on Self-Deception* (Berkeley: University of California Press, 1988), pp. 157–69.

may well be all the more difficult to correct, when spotted in others, because it develops largely as an unreflective habit rather than by a conscious decision.

Self-deceit may also vary in the extent to which it is irrational. Clearly it must always involve some element of *cognitive* impropriety, in that the self-deceiver is not being honest with himself about the evidence and what it indicates. That is certainly one kind of irrationality. But, if we look at the *purpose* of self-deceit, we find that it is not necessarily irrational though it may in practice often be so. The man who has deceived himself in thinking that his beloved returns his affection is certainly going to be much more upset by the news that she has finally married someone else than the man who all along had doubts about his chances. So, if the motivation for his self-deceit was to avoid the pain of rejection, he chose the wrong course of action. If he had made a more rational appreciation of the situation, he would have avoided the temptation to self-deceit in order to reconcile himself to the possibility of losing his beloved. In that way he would have reduced whatever suffering he might have to endure in the end. But sometimes the pain of an accepted truth may be unendurable and the only recourse then, bar intoxication or suicide, is self-deceit. In those circumstances self-deceit seems to be quite rationally motivated. Perhaps, for example, that is how a convinced but charitable atheist may view the failure of intellectually sophisticated theists to give up their religion in the face of terrible natural disasters. Their religion, without which life is unendurable to them, requires them to accept the existence of an omniscient, omnipotent, and benevolent deity. So, according to the atheist, they deceive themselves into accepting this by suppressing their intellectual worries about the countervailing evidence that is constituted by natural disasters. And perhaps such a form of self-deceit is not irrational, the charitable atheist may think, so far as its purpose is to make life endurable for those who practise it.

In any paradox in which an antinomy is generated—for example, where it is proved that an arrow moves and also that it is stationary, or that a particular set both is and is not a member of itself—the paradox can be resolved only when we reject or modify one or more assumptions that are essential for the reasoning by which the antinomy is generated. Different resolutions of the paradox require different assumptions to be rejected or modified.

And the best resolution is the one that changes assumptions in the least objectionable way. So we find that the self-command analysis of self-deception, and the analysis in terms of rival criteria, both require us to exclude an accusation of self-deceit from implying that the self-deceiver is intellectually dishonest—which would emasculate the accusation. Moreover, a two-systems analysis excludes us from assuming that the deceiver and the deceived are one and the same individual, exercising the usual range of cognitive abilities; and, if we cannot assume this, self-deceit is impossible. But, if we can exploit the distinction between belief and acceptance (which is in any case needed for other purposes), the only assumption that we have to drop, in order to make our description of self-deception consistent, is the appropriateness of using the same term, such as 'thinking', to describe both the involuntary cognitive attitude in virtue of which the agent is a deceiver and also the voluntary cognitive attitude that he is deceived into adopting. Instead we need to use in these roles some such pair of terms as 'belief' and 'acceptance', respectively, and then the antinomy can no longer be constructed, since belief that p and acceptance that p are logically independent of one another.

Of course, all that has been shown above is that self-deceit is logically possible, not that it is psychologically possible—let alone that it actually occurs. *If* self-deceit occurs, that is what it is like. So, however much accusations of self-deceit are bandied about, we are left with the question whether they may not be too extravagant to be true. In particular, by any such accusation the self-deceiver is credited with a good deal of unconscious mental activity. What is implied is that the desire that p unconsciously but effectively motivates him to misinterpret the relevant evidence and to suppress his belief that not-p in favour of accepting that p. So he is implied to be unconscious of his own motivation in the matter and of his misinterpretation of the evidence, and also of his own underlying belief. Now it is often difficult enough to be sure even of what is going on in another person's conscious mind. We have to infer his private thoughts from what he reports to us about them or from his overt behaviour. But the difficulties are much greater when we seek knowledge about what is going on in his *un*conscious mind —on which he *ex hypothesi* cannot report. Perhaps it would be less extravagant to theorize, for example, that every supposed case of self-deceit is really no more than a case of wishful thinking and lacks any suppression of an opposed belief. Indeed, the very existence of unconscious mental activity is not an empirical discovery but an explanatory postulate. And it is a postulate that is by no means a commonplace in every human culture or folk psychology, as an examination of ancient Greco-Roman literature, for example, soon makes clear.

But fortunately the existence of self-deceit on this or that occasion, or its psychological possibility in general, is not an issue in the present context. I have been arguing instead about conceptual analysis and logical possibility. And my claim is just that a distinction between belief and acceptance is vital for the correct analysis of the concept of self-deceit, whether or not that concept is ever satisfied. Self-deceit is one possible species of a type of mental state that is also conceptually admissible in certain other contexts (§3, §§7–12, §§13–15, §§16–22). It is one of the ways in which what a person accepts may differ from what he believes.

§26. SOME PROPOSED RESOLUTIONS OF THE SOCRATIC PARADOX

Several philosophers[17] have pointed out that the lack of moral self-control which Aristotle called *akrasia*[18] can be viewed as analogous in certain respects to self-deception. In *akrasia*, it is said, the agent is subject to two opposing states of mind about what he should do, just as in self-deception the agent is subject to a conflict between two opposing states of mind about what is the case. Thus, in a typical instance a man, who in his own conscience fully endorses the maxim not to drink three whiskies and then drive, nevertheless succumbs to the temptation to drink a third whisky before driving away from the party. And succumbing to one such form of temptation or another is surely a familiar, recognizable kind of occurrence. Yet its description seems at first sight to involve a contradiction. We apparently have to say, in regard to the proposed

---

[17] For example, D. F. Pears, *Motivated Irrationality*, pp. 24–40, and A. R. Mele, *Irrationality: An Essay on Akrasia, Self-Control* (New York: Oxford University Press, 1987), p. ix.

[18] *Nicomachean Ethics*, bk. VII. It is unnecessary for present purposes to follow through all the details of Aristotle's discussion. We are dealing with a certain type of ethical paradox, whatever the history of its recognition.

example, both that the agent does not want his third drink and that he does want it, much as in describing a case of self-deceit we seemed to have to say both that the agent *A* does not think that *p* and also that he does think that *p*. So how is this further paradox to be resolved? What we should expect, if the analogy between self-deceit and *akrasia* is anything to go by, is that the kind of solution that succeeds for self-deceit succeeds also for *akrasia* as thus understood. And so it turns out. Of course, on any understanding of the matter there are also elements of disanalogy between self-deceit and *akrasia*. In particular, when *akrasia* is attributed to someone nothing is implied thereby about unconscious mental states or processes. But these disanalogies will not affect the substance of the issue.

Consider first the Socratic position—that no one errs willingly. On this view a person who knows the right way to act will always act rightly so far as it is within his power to do so.[19] The agent's mind cannot then be the forum for a conflict between two opposing maxims for voluntary action—a morally correct maxim and a morally incorrect one—and the paradox disappears. And this approach to the paradox is sometimes reinforced by the argument that since we should infer the maxims that a person thinks correct from what he does voluntarily rather than from what he says (since he may be speaking hypocritically), we can never have any evidence of his being in a state of *akrasia*.

We may compare here the attempt to solve the paradox of self-deception by viewing it as a case of self-command. But, just as in any such case of self-command no contrary command is also supposed, so too the Socratic approach to *akrasia* rules out any scenario in which opposing maxims conflict with one another in the agent's mind. It therefore fails to represent the familiar type of situation that is intuitively felt to set a problem. In particular it allows no room for the occurrence of remorse to make sense. Remorse is only appropriate where one has voluntarily followed a course of action that conflicts with a maxim or maxims that one thinks to be right. But according to the Socratic approach no such course of action can be voluntary.

Another well-known treatment of *akrasia*, due to Davidson,[20]

---

[19] For an example of such a thesis see R. M. Hare, *Freedom and Reason* (Oxford: Clarendon Press, 1963), pp. 77 ff.

[20] D. Davidson, *Actions and Events* (Oxford: Clarendon Press, 1982), pp. 21 ff.

tends to trivialize the issue. It exploits the difference between generalizations that hold always and unconditionally, and generalizations that hold normally and when other things are equal. So the conflict in *akrasia* between a moral and a hedonic maxim is allegedly not to be viewed as a formal contradiction but merely as an opposition between two prima facie guiding principles. Which principle is to prevail is a question that the agent has to answer in the light of all relevant considerations. And a parallel may be drawn here, we are told,[21] with conditional probabilities. The probability that George will die before the age of 40 given that he's a farmer may be low, and the probability that he will die before the age of 40 given that he's a hang-glider may be high. But these two probabilities are not at all irreconcilable, since the probability that he will actually die before the age of 40 has to be determined in the light of *all* his relevant circumstances. Moreover, on Davidson's view, the two guiding principles may both be moral ones or both be non-moral ones. It does not have to be the case that one has the status of a moral norm and the other does not.

This proposal for the analysis of *akrasia*, as the parallelism with conditional probability helps to make clear, is like treating self-deceit as arising merely from a conflict between different criteria of evidential appraisal. That treatment of self-deceit understated the sharpness, and trivialized the nature, of the conflict between opposing thoughts by ignoring altogether the element of intellectual dishonesty that is necessary for one criterion to come to prevail over the other. In self-deceit a thought has to be dishonestly suppressed, because it cannot be honestly reconciled with its opponent. So too the corresponding treatment of *akrasia* understates the sharpness, and trivializes the nature, of the conflict that must exist between the two maxims if the agent is later to be in a position to experience justifiable remorse. The agent gets to be in such a position only because in the given situation there is no way of decently reconciling the two maxims with one another. There *is* a wrong maxim, indeed a morally wrong one, and the agent acts voluntarily and knowingly in accordance with it.

A connected flaw in Davidson's analysis of *akrasia* is that, because it sees *akrasia* as being merely a conflict between prima facie principles, it makes the question of motivation irrelevant and

---

[21] Ibid. p. 37.

seeks to establish a contrast thereby with self-deceit, in which the agent's motivation is certainly an integral issue.[22] But in fact *akrasia* integrally requires, as Aristotle long ago saw,[23] that the agent's diversion from the moral to the hedonic maxim be motivated by a desire for pleasure or for the avoidance of distress.

In view of these difficulties a two-systems analysis is superficially attractive here. A conscience-dominated system is then seen to be fighting it out with a pleasure-dominated system. In such a battle two maxims are in genuine opposition to one another and no compromise or reconciliation is supposed to be possible. At least that feature of *akrasia* is modelled in the analysis.

But here too, as with the two-systems analysis of self-deceit, there is an *ignoratio elenchi*. What lies at the heart of the problem is that just one person is involved, not two or three. So the depiction of two different motivational systems fighting one another for the control of some physical mechanism, like a human body, is inherently inappropriate as a description of the situation. After all, the person who may feel remorse has certainly to be the same as the one who hears the dictates of his conscience. But he also has to be the same as the one who experiences the illicit pleasure. So the person who has a conscience, the person who experiences pleasure, and the person who may feel remorse are one and the same person, with a single motivational history. That is essential to the conceptual possibility of *akrasia*.

§27. *AKRASIA* AS A CASE OF ACCEPTANCE DOMINATING BELIEF

None of these difficulties arise, however, if we exploit the distinction between belief and acceptance appropriately. We have here yet another type of case in which acceptance does not coincide with belief. Let us assume, schematically, that the agent has a moral belief that requires him to bring it about that not-p, while he self-indulgently accepts as his maxim the principle of bringing it about that p. His conscience firmly dictates that he should bring it about that not-p, but he prefers to satisfy his desire that p. It is

---

[22] Cf. Davidson, 'Deception and Division', p. 142.
[23] *Nicomachean Ethics*, bk. VIII, ch. iv (1147b20 ff.).

clear then that the two relevant maxims, between which he has consciously to decide, can formally contradict one another. For example, the maxim not to drink three whiskies and then drive may be imposed on the agent by his moral beliefs, while the maxim prescribing a third drink before he drives is the one that, because of its pleasure-value, and his strong desire to act in conformity with it, he accepts as his premiss for guidance in the actual situation. Thus the moral backsliding is conceived of as being fully voluntary, since acceptance is always voluntary. The desire was not a pathological, uncontrollable one (see §8 above). And this voluntariness is quite important here since it leaves room for the possibility that the agent may come to feel justified remorse about the direction that his deliberations took: there is no room for remorse about something that is inherently involuntary. But at the same time the moral maxim is the object of a belief, which is involuntary. And that involuntariness also has an appropriate part to play in modelling the *akrasia* situation, because even though the moral maxim does not prevail, the agent cannot rid himself of belief in its inherent rightness. Nor can he even suppress this belief, as in self-deceit. Indeed, it is the agent's continued disposition to feel it true that he ought not to drink three whiskies and then drive that may conceivably generate a moment of remorse as he downs the third glass.

Of course, there is still a difference between, on the one hand, accepting that one should bring it about that *p*, because of its superior pleasurableness, and, on the other hand, actually bringing it about that *p*. After all, people often resist temptation and may be given due credit for so doing. But the paradox of *akrasia* is an analytical, not a psychological, problem and requires us to show how *akrasia* is conceptually possible, not how it is causally possible (just as we had to unravel a conceptual and not a causal possibility in the case of self-deceit). What is thus essential is to show how an agent's belief that he is not to do a particular act may be consistent with his acceptance that he is to do it. The voluntary bodily action that eventually takes place is just the natural outcome of this voluntary act of acceptance in the mind. That is to say, the occurrence of the bodily action is fully explained—in the circumstances—by the mental act of acceptance.

It is also worth noting that *akrasia*, like self-deceit, may be seen to be not inherently irrational when the appropriate distinction between belief and acceptance has dissolved the antinomy whereby a person may apparently be shown both to want and not to want the same thing. It is, for example, certainly immoral to put other people's lives seriously at risk for the sake of one's own passing pleasures. But there is nothing inherently irrational about this, except in the context of some philosophical theory, like Kant's or Plato's, that analyses morality in terms of rationality. On the other hand, it is generally considered irrational—irrespective of any philosophical theory—to sacrifice important elements in your own long-term interests for the sake of unimportant elements in your short-term ones. It would be irrational to run a serious risk of ending up a paraplegic, for example, just for the sake of a third whisky. So *akrasia* is irrational in everyday terms only so far as it involves some such risk or folly. Or, in other words, when an *akrasia*-generated action happens also to be irrational, it is not the *akrasia*, but some other, independent circumstance of the action, that makes it irrational.

But can an *akrasia*-generated action be not only not irrational but actually rational? Though it is clear that some cases of self-deceit are rationally motivated in that they serve to rescue the self-deceiver from unendurable anxiety or depression (as we saw in §25), it is not so obvious that there are any analogous cases of *akrasia*. Perhaps such cases do exist in relation to moral codes that demand extreme self-sacrifice from people under certain circumstances. If you have a moral duty to risk death in order to protect your country's flag from dishonour, for instance, it may be more rational to look the other way while it is burned. But the more such situations are treated instead as occasions for the exercise of supererogatory virtue, rather than of moral duty, the easier it is for a person's moral duty to be seen as being in line with what is rational. In short, where the standards of duty are lower, it is easier for morality and rationality to march together.

§28. COULD SELF-DECEIT OR *AKRASIA* BE A CASE OF
BELIEF DOMINATING ACCEPTANCE?

We saw earlier (in §25) that the paradox of self-deception disappears when we cease to regard the same term ('thinking', say) as appropriate for describing both the type of cognitive attitude that the agent has in his role as deceiver and also the type of cognitive attitude that he has in his role as deceived. And it has now become clear (in §27) that the paradox of *akrasia* disappears when we cease to regard the same term ('wanting', say) as appropriate for describing both the agent's type of attitude towards following the maxim dictated by his conscience and also his type of attitude towards following the maxim dictated by his desire for pleasure. When we see the nature of the difference between the two types of attitude involved—that is, the difference between belief and acceptance, respectively—the paradox disappears in both cases.

Someone may object that seeing the difference between this pair of attitudes is sufficient for the resolution of the paradoxes and that we do not have to suppose that it is the same member of the pair that plays the same role in every case. Thus I have argued that in self-deception the suppressed thought is a belief, while the usurping thought is one that is accepted, and that analogously in *akrasia* to have a maxim endorsed by a conscience is to have a belief, while succumbing to the temptations of a maxim that conflicts with conscience is an act of acceptance. The objector may claim that these roles can be reversed, and that the suppressed thought or defeated maxim may be generated originally by an act of acceptance, while the usurping thought or winning maxim is a kind of belief. So long as the two different kinds of mental attitudes involved are logically independent of one another, he may say, there is no reason why they should not coexist in the mind of a single person despite their opposition to one another. It does not matter which is the dominating one and which is the dominated one, just so long as two different kinds of attitude are involved. Firm belief that *p* always sits awkwardly with firm belief that not-*p*, and acceptance that *p* with acceptance that not-*p*. What resolves the paradox is just the recognition that the same cognitive function does not have thus to be attributed mutually opposed states at the same time. Indeed, Dennett has proposed[24] a resolution of the paradoxes in which it is the usurping thought or winning maxim that is a matter of belief, while the suppressed thought or defeated maxim is what he calls an 'opinion', where opinion is like acceptance in differing from belief in being active, always linguistically

[24] D. Dennett, *Brainstorms: Philosophical Essays on Mind and Psychology* (Hassocks: Harvester Press, 1979), pp. 306–7.

formulatable, a matter of degree, and not available to animals. (Although there are also important differences between opinion and acceptance—pp. 15–16 above—these need not concern us here.)

However, Dennett's type of proposal for resolving the paradoxes will not work. Consider self-deceit first, and for that purpose look again at its model—ordinary, two-party deceit. In the latter, A has to *believe* that not-*p* if there is to be any dishonesty in his persuading B to think that *p*. Otherwise, if A wants B to think that *p*, A could simply accept that *p* for the purpose and there would then be no discrepancy between A's own state and the one that he wants B to adopt. Similarly, in self-deceit there has to be a rock-bottom belief that not-*p*, which the man who deceives himself that *p* can only suppress but not eradicate. If all that is unwelcome to him in his current mental state is that he accepts that not-*p* when he would prefer to accept that *p* he can simply change his mind, cease to accept that not-*p*, and accept that *p* instead. But if he has to cope with a belief that not-*p* the sheer involuntariness of belief excludes any such easy relief and he has to adopt the elaborate strategies of self-deception. The thesis that the self-deceiver believes, deep down, that not-*p* coheres with the supposition of an unconsciously felt desire for self-deceit, whereas the thesis that he accepts that not-*p* does not.

Moreover, the mental state at which the self-deceiver arrives has to be thought of as voluntarily adopted, if he is to be open to the accusation of intellectual folly that is implicit in the charge of self-deceit. He has to let himself be deceived—and by himself, of all people! But what a person does involuntarily is not a folly of any kind. So the hypothesis that the self-deceiver comes to accept that *p* can explain the conceptual legitimacy of our disparaging him in this way, whereas the hypothesis that he believes that *p* cannot. Indeed, we should note the fact that in two-party deceit the normal purpose of the exercise is that the deceived person should accept the false proposition—i.e. take it as a premiss for his decisions and deliberations—whether or not he comes also to have the corresponding mistaken belief. And, however difficult it may sometimes be in practice, he can in principle always resist deception. That is, it makes sense to attribute to the deceived party the option of rejecting the false proposition. So too the characteristic purpose of *self*-deceit is that the dominating, deceiving thought should be voluntarily adopted as an available premiss for consolation, gratification, deliberation, etc. Self-deception would be pointless unless it issued in some such act of acceptance. The self-deceiver puts things wrong in order to get things wrong. Hence it is the dominating wrong thought, not the dominated right one, that has to be attributed to an act of acceptance. The self-deceiver may even pretend to himself—as to others—that he believes that *p*, but he does not really believe that *p*.

Again, we can point to the fact that the typical self-deceiver is credited with acknowledging an obligation to defend every perceived implication of his dominating thought that *p*. If George's dominating thought is that Mary loves him, then, in order to explain why Mary went the other way in the street yesterday, he takes it that she failed to see him. Everything has to be made to fit the prepared picture. So the self-deceiver is conceived of as taking his dominating thought to be subjectively closed under deducibility. And the explanation of this must be that he is conceived to accept the dominating thought, since it is acceptance, not belief, that is subjectively closed under deducibility.

Finally, it is always at least logically possible for the self-deceiver to break out of his self-made web of deception. He is in principle able to sift carefully through all the relevant evidence and to monitor rigorously and honestly all the inferences that he draws from it. So in the end he may deprive himself of any evidential reason to accept that *p* and may instead come to recognize adequate evidential reason to accept his previously suppressed belief that not-*p*. Of course, in practice a self-deceiver is not always strong-willed enough to face reality in this way, overcoming whatever motivation existed for his self-deceit. But, if he does end up by putting things right, it will be by just such a switchover in what he accepts, thus confirming that his previously dominating wrong thought should be attributed to a voluntary act of acceptance, not to a passive state of belief. These points are valid also against Bach's analysis[25] (along with the earlier argument against Bach— on p. 144—about how the self-deceiver handles the evidence). Bach recognizes that the dominated thought is suppressed belief. But he regards the dominating thought as an uncontrollable occurrence in the mind of the self-deceiver, like the experience of the person who

[25] Bach, 'An Analysis of Self-Deception', pp. 351–70.

'cannot help thinking that flying is dangerous'.[26] Clearly this can account neither for the voluntariness nor for the deductive closure of the dominating thought. And the same points count against Elster's and Davidson's view that self-deceit requires the simultaneous entertainment of incompatible beliefs.[27]

No doubt there are occasions on which a person, who once believed that not-*p*, may correctly be stated to have deceived himself into believing that *p*. But even then we do not have a case of self-deceit in which the dominating thought is a belief. The implication on these occasions is rather that the process by which the thinker has arrived at his present state of mind, not that state itself, is an instance of self-deceit. Perhaps he deceived himself about what the evidence was or about what it indicated. And now he has lost, not merely suppressed, his earlier belief that not-*p*. For that is the distinctive implication of saying that he has deceived himself into believing that *p*, as against saying something like, 'He is deceiving himself in thinking that *p*.'[28] Of course, the person who has suppressed (while still unconsciously retaining) his belief that not-*p* and has accepted self-deceivingly that *p*, may actually come to believe that he believes that *p*. But this kind of belief, far from being correct, is itself a by-product of the self-deception and increases the difficulty of a person's undeceiving himself. It tends to camouflage his responsibility for the mental state that he is in.

In *akrasia* analogous arguments apply. A person is to blame for siding with some pleasure-seeking maxim when his conscience reminds him of his duty. So this siding is the voluntary mental act for which he is held responsible and may later feel remorse. Accordingly, any such succumbing to temptation can be classified as an act of acceptance. And any mental exercise of self-control, whereby the admonitions of conscience come to dominate over the temptations of pleasure, is also classifiable as an act of acceptance because it is similarly voluntary. To exercise self-control you need to *decide* to exert an appropriate effort, just as you may need to do

---

[26] Ibid. p. 357.

[27] J. Elster, *Ulysses and the Sirens* (Cambridge: Cambridge University Press, 1979), p. 174; and D. Davidson, 'Deception and Division', p. 147.

[28] So the paradox of self-deceit cannot be resolved by taking self-deceit to be a temporally scattered event, as suggested by R. A. Sorensen, 'Self-Deception and Scattered Events', *Mind*, 94 (1985), pp. 64–9. Sorensen's analysis fits being deceived *into* believing, not being deceived *in* believing.

in order to be honest with yourself and avoid self-deceit. The admonitions of conscience themselves, however, are involuntary, so, whether accepted or rejected, they may be seen as manifestations of moral belief, and not, *pace* Dennett,[29] of acceptance, judgement, or opinion.

[29] *Brainstorms*, pp. 308–9.

INDEX